RISK FROM THE CEO
AND BOARD
PERSPECTIVE

RISK FROM THE CEO AND BOARD PERSPECTIVE

Mary Pat McCarthy
and
Timothy P. Flynn

Contributing author:
Rob Brownstein

McGraw-Hill

New York Chicago San Francisco Lisbon London
Madrid Mexico City Milan New Delhi San Juan
Seoul Singapore Sydney Toronto

3 4 5 6 7 8 9 0 AGM/AGM 0 9 8 7 6 5 4

ISBN 0-07-143471-2

Printed and bound by Quebecor World.

Contents

Acknowledgments

S itting down to write a book is a proposition filled with risk, but we were rewarded beyond our due by the gracious consideration and support that so many people gave to this project. We are indebted to each of these individuals and know with certainty this book is better for their help.

To General Barry McCaffrey, for his insights on the greatest risks of all, those played out in the field of battle.

To the 15 executives and board members who graciously shared their time and experiences with us: Richard Bressler, Senior Executive Vice President and CFO of Viacom; Brent Callinicos, Corporate Vice President and Treasurer of Microsoft; Doh-Seok Choi, President and CFO of Samsung; Jeff Clarke, Executive Vice President of Global Operations of Hewlett-Packard; Robert Dellinger, Executive Vice President and CFO of Sprint; Scott Di Valerio, Corporate Vice President and Corporate Controller of Microsoft; Pattie Dunn, Vice Chairman of Barclays Global Investors and a member of Hewlett-Packard's Board of Directors; Rod Eddington, CEO of British Airways; Jeff Henley, Executive Vice President and CFO of Oracle; Mark Hurd, CEO of NCR; Jay Keyworth, Chairman of the Progress & Freedom Foundation and a member of Hewlett-Packard's Board of

Directors; Peter Oppenheimer, Senior Vice President of Finance and Corporate Controller of Apple Computer; Ken West, Chairman of the Board of the National Association of Corporate Directors, former CEO of Harris Bankcorp, member of the Board of Directors of Motorola and The Pepper Companies, and the Senior Consultant for Corporate Governance at TIAA/CREF; Robert Woods, CBE, CEO of P&O Group; and John Wren, CEO of Omnicom Group.

To our partners and colleagues, for the wisdom and assistance they so generously gave: Stephen Allis, Amy Beard, Tim Bell, Donna Bonavita, Alun Bowen, Darryl Briley, Stuart Campbell, Mark Carleton, Michael Conover, Frederic Cooper, Malcolm Dahn, Patricia Derry, Jonathan Eesley, Patty Eisenbarth, Bob Elliott, Carl Geppert, Terrence Henzey, Ted Horne, Diane Kiffin-Nardin, Peter Kim, Dut LeBlanc, Neil Lerner, Gary Lord, Lisa Madden, Dale LeMasters, Gary Matuszak, Young Jin Park, Tim Pearson, Scott Reed, Chris Rice, Greg Russo, Terri Santisi, Phil Schimmel, Ted Senko, Richard Smith, Charlie Steadman, Ashley Steel, Ron Steger, Claudia Taft, Mark Terrell, Dabie Tsai-Blake, Joseph Verga, YG "Ken" Yun, and Hiroaki Yoshihara.

To the steadfast support of Rob Brownstein and McGraw-Hill, and to Marie Glenn, for her assistance in researching, writing and producing this book.

Mary Pat McCarthy
Timothy Flynn
November 2003

Introduction

If you knew in 1998 what you know now, what would your company have done differently? No doubt the answers run from limiting debt financing, to paying a lot more attention to cash generation, to much more focus on bottom- rather than top-line results. But no one would say, "I wouldn't change a thing."

The early Greeks and Romans didn't worry about uncertainty. Though they had the mathematical skills to have conceived and developed ways of analyzing probabilities, it didn't occur to them to try. The very idea of uncertainty would have been foreign. They believed that everything was predestined. It wasn't until the Middle Ages that the idea of probability arose and rigorous attempts at analysis occurred. Within a couple of centuries the pendulum had swung so far that many believed every system could be precisely analyzed in probability terms. Humanity had thus developed the concept of "uncertainty," and began applying its skills to sorting the odds.

Fast forward to 2003. In the five years from 1998, a booming economy has flip-flopped and been languishing for almost three years. U.S. public company capitalization, particularly in the technology sector, is a fraction of what it was in

2000. A general strike in Venezuela coupled with growing fears of renewed hostilities in the Middle East caused a sharp spike in petroleum prices. The September 11, 2001, attacks on the United States and Middle Eastern unrest has put a damper on travel, further depressing an already troubled airline and tourism industry. A corona virus usually associated with diseases in fowl jumped species to humans in China and sparked a pandemic that spread from Asia to North America. In its wake, some of the countries involved—China (including Hong Kong), Vietnam, Singapore, and Canada—issued travel warnings and imposed strict quarantines on those believed to have been exposed. In March 2003 the United States and the United Kingdom began a preemptive war with Iraq, the military outcome of which was all but certain, but for which the postwar scenarios abound with uncertainty.

What do travel restrictions and quarantines do to companies that depend upon Singapore for hard-disk-drive manufacturing? What do higher petroleum prices do to operating costs of airlines and package-delivery companies? What do sagging share prices do to the cost of funding for public companies? What's the possibility of a massive earthquake on California's Hayward fault causing severe damage to Silicon Valley's technology business infrastructure? Can the outbreak of disease in Taiwan hobble the supply of key components and force electronic system production to come to a screeching halt? Will the postwar events in Iraq tend to stabilize or destabilize the fragile geopolitics of the Middle East? What effect will it have on petroleum supply and pricing, on global economics, on relations between the United States and the

United Nations, and on the domestic U.S. economy and national government?

When trying to get a handle on your company's exposure to unexpected events, how do you factor in wars, terrorism, natural disasters, epidemics, economic turmoil, and political upheavals? How do you decide which risks to avoid, which to try and mitigate, and which to accept in your effort to optimize shareholder value?

According to General Barry McCaffrey, who provided strategic and tactical analyses for NBC during the military phase of Operation Iraqi Freedom, and whom we interviewed in writing this book: "We actually came very close to having a disaster in Iraq. We essentially got almost none of our maintenance management system through in the advance from the south of Iraq toward Baghdad. Had the Iraqis fought in Baghdad as they did in Al Nasyriyah, Basra, and elsewhere, we would have had a political and military disaster." McCaffrey felt that the Secretary of Defense and his military advisers had underestimated the risks associated with supply and maintenance. And, by holding fast to a relatively small number of combatants to be engaged at the outset, the military and Secretary of Defense were trading off a potentially serious risk to prove a point about military efficiency.

As we pointed out in *Agile Business for Fragile Times*, it is important to determine which factors you can control and which you cannot. In *Security Transformation*, we showed how to avoid spending more on security than the value of the information you were trying to protect. These lessons can be transferred to issues surrounding risk. In this case, though, eliminating the risk is only one option. Good risk management is really choice management. What do you want to do? Do you want to avoid the risk, hedge it, or optimize it? The answer depends partly on deciding the degree of risk your company is willing to assume. There, it is important not only to look at the tangible consequences—like the percent change in currency exchange rates and its effect on revenues—but to the intangible possibilities, such as investor perception of currency fluctuation on business results.

The venerable New York Yankee catcher Yogi Berra once said, "The future ain't what it used to be." Many people today are saying the level of uncertainty has never been higher. This may or may not be true, but certainly the pace and penetration of communications has changed. Latency—the time it takes for information to ripple through from source to recipient—has gotten much shorter. That speed, coupled with prevailing perceptions, can precipitate huge movements in a securities, bonds, or commodities market, which in turn may have a significant effect upon a national or global economy.

For example, in the pre-Enron era, a company's announcement of revenue restatement may have caused downward pressure on its share prices, but perhaps not as precipitous as is likely to happen in today's post-Enron era. The information speed of the announcements involved are comparable, but the perceptions of those who act upon that information are very different. When latencies were much longer, it tended to have a dampening effect upon knee-jerk reactions. Now, with today's nearly instant information dissemination, the perception issue is often the larger factor in trying to assess positive or negative consequences.

There is a tendency to want to compartmentalize risks and sort them into distinct, mutually exclusive categories. The underlying assumption is that the consequences of the unforeseen event will more or less be confined to a given area—financial or operational, for example. In actuality, the fallout from unforeseen events tends to affect multiple business areas, and it may make more sense to take a holistic view of risks, factoring in interdependencies.

Either things are indeed more uncertain today than they've ever been before, or it just seems that way because of the speed and penetration of information stimulus and response. In either case, you are obligated to shareholders and other stakeholders to blend whatever quantitative handholds you can find with a systematic approach to risk management that mixes data, experience, logic, and intuition to optimize positive results.

Risk management is unquestionably a work in progress. This book is a look at what some of your peers are thinking and doing about risk today. It explores ways of organizing ourselves to best assess and manage risk. In addition, it looks at how closely coupled or integrated risk should be in business, operational, and financial planning, and how you might use this knowledge to a shareholder's and stakeholder's advantage.

We hope you enjoy.

RISK FROM THE CEO
AND BOARD
PERSPECTIVE

Companies
at Risk

CHAPTER 1

Executive Agenda

*"If everything seems under control, you're just
not going fast enough."*

—Mario Andretti

A great many approaches for discussing and modeling
risk have been born over the years, in many cases
springing from discrete industry or functional concerns.
This has led risk management to be perceived as an arcane,
technical subject germane to financial risk managers with an
appetite for actuarial mathematics. This book suggests
otherwise. We believe the business of risk management is
undergoing a fundamental sea change. At the tiller are CEOs
and boards that have been awash in a roiling surge of new or
emerging risk realities for over a year. From them, it is clear
that more than ever the risk discipline is converging at the
top of the organization, linked inextricably to strategy and
stakeholders.

Risk from the CEO and Board Perspective is a response to
these changes. It is designed as a primer for senior corporate

management to streamline the many diverse threads that exist on the subject, and to focus attention on the key risk questions and considerations.

We'll begin with an agenda for leadership; a look at some things to come and at changes already underway in boards and executive suites around the world.

OVERVIEW OF COLLECTIVE WISDOM

The views in this section, gathered from our conversations with CEOs and board members, illustrate some of the higher-level thoughts and issues being discussed and championed today. Together, they demonstrate that meaningful dialogue on risk management is occurring, and they highlight a growing sensibility of the transformation of risk management from conformance to performance.

What Can Bring Your Business Down?

One of the board's primary tasks is to understand and approve both the risk appetite at current and future stages of evolution and to understand the monitoring processes in place that keep risk and risk appetite in alignment. Among their considerations, boards need to ask themselves how much risk the company can absorb. They need to ask questions like:

☐ "Are you okay if some risks can't be controlled?"

☐ "Are you overcomplying or undercomplying with the recent slate of regulations?"

☐ "How much is that costing you?"

☐ "Are your PR offices poised to handle crisis management effectively when intangibles like reputation and brand take a hit?"

☐ "Is the management of these intangibles factored into your business continuity plans?"

We know even more keenly now that damage to a company's integrity can fell an organization if enough blows are sustained. Yet, many businesses have still to formally assess how much risk their company can or should absorb, and their risk conversations suffer for that.

Robert Woods, CEO of shipping and container giant P&O, says: "We do quarterly reforecasts for our business with the board, and at those reforecasts, we talk about the major variables to our risk analysis, the variables to our cargo flow, growth, oil prices, currency swings, and the like. But the major point of emphasis, the major thing we discuss, is the question of what can destroy our forecast? What can bring the business down?"

Risk Is the Art of Balancing Interests

Corporations are not democracies, but the right separation of powers is important to balance every group's self-interest. Formal partitioning of the Chairman and Chief Executive offices will be advocated by some to allow for greater oversight and impartiality. Others will prefer to add nonexecutive or outside directors to provide the needed objectivity and perspective.

Within the organization, many executives agree that the process of reporting, measuring, and controlling risks should be managed separately and independently from those who generate them. Just as an independent board, audit committee, and auditor are critical to effective corporate governance, an independent risk management function is essential to effective operations. Complex multinationals may decide that a separate risk management team is required. Smaller companies may designate a member of management not involved with the day-to-day activities that might generate risk for the company. Independence is advanced when the company's organizational, reporting, and compensation structure are properly aligned in support of it.

The CEO and Board Are Ulitmately Responsible

Jay Keyworth, chairman of the Progress & Freedom Foundation and a member of Hewlett-Packard's board, states: "I think the most important lesson of the last few years is that board members can no longer dismiss being knowledgeable about business risk." He's saying that when something goes wrong—and it inevitably will—you will be held accountable.

The solution is not only to make sure that you learn of adverse risk conditions, but that you are sufficiently attuned to the environments that generate these conditions in the first place, and in time to take preemptive action. Understand what red flags can derail your strategy and, just as important, can derail the execution of that strategy. Then make sure you have a mechanism in place to alert you if those flags start waving.

You Don't Have to Be a Bean Counter, But You Need to Understand the Numbers

The CFO may be the top accountant, but every board member has a responsibility to understand accounting basics. Many do not. Two-thirds of the executives at a recent University of Chicago course on corporate governance—many from Fortune 500 companies—failed to correctly answer a multiple-choice question on retained earnings. Although audit committees in particular need a thorough knowledge of the company and its industry, the board as a whole must understand the financial instruments the company uses and owns, and be familiar with the control environments in place.

Have an Exit Strategy

While management and boards may have disaster recovery procedures to protect and back up key assets, they need to bring the same contingency planning to their strategic discussions. An exit strategy and plan is essential when considering any large scale initiative or transformation.

Peter Oppenheimer, Apple Computer's SVP of Finance, has made this his credo: "Companies should only take risks that they have the core competencies and skills to manage, have clearly thought through, including an exit strategy, and that are strategically aligned with their business." He adds: "When you go into something new, it has to be really well thought out, and if for some reason it doesn't work out, you have to know what the back door is."

This is true of most strategic undertakings, but is particularly prudent when embarking on any type of merger or acquisition. Given managers' proclivity to keep their sights trained on the next deal, this can be hard to do. Success involves discipline, and lots of it. Otherwise, when you take on more individual risks than you have the capacity to manage, Oppenheimer notes, "You get yourself into trouble."

Good Disclosure Lies in What,
Not How Much, Is Revealed

Many executives agree that there is too much emphasis on the quantity of disclosure and too little on the quality of information being disclosed. To achieve quality disclosure, there must be an underlying infrastructure that produces accurate information and is supported by adequate controls and fundamentally sound business operations.

Investors, we know, are not always helped by reams of pages to pore through. They are looking for clear, concise information, not just data. Yet, the emphasis on reporting and transparency can cloud the areas of strategic risk that should attract the most attention—questions such as: What are the competitive challenges we face? What and where do we invest? What risks threaten to overcome our objectives and strategies We talk about financial reporting risk, but financial reporting risk starts with strategic planning.

Organizations Need a Structured Approach
to Risk Management

Ironically, while most CEOs and boards have all sorts of sophisticated systems for managing other aspects of their business, risk management is often done intuitively. Many now recognize that the time is ripe for processes and owner-ship to be formalized, to better and more reliably handle critical aspects of the business. The question is: Where to start?

Some advisers recommend an annual two-day off-site in which CEOs and management convene exclusively on the subject of risk and risk management, away from the day-to-day distractions of business. Back at the shop, strategic or enterprise risk management, as it is variously called, offers what many leaders consider the best approach to cohesively discuss, model, and understand risk. This is viewed as an effective vehicle for gathering, "in one place," insight on total business risk—historical, future, and compliance risk—which also allows for efficient continual assessment, a factor missing from many current corporate approaches.

The Mirror Reflects Only One View of Reality

CEOs and boards of directors often have an overly optimistic sense of corporate self. Ken West, former CEO of Harris Bankcorp and a member of Motorola's Audit Committee, says: "Many companies tend to look at the world through rose-colored glasses. They say if our markets grow on at eight to 10 percent, we'll grow at 12 to 15 percent. And if the competition's operating margins are 10 percent, we can do 12 percent, even though we're now doing five percent." Is that a risk? West asks rhetorically. "Sure!" he says. "I think that's a risk because boards frequently tend to accept company-generated projections without challenging the underlying assumptions. All too often they don't think about all the factors that could prevent those results from being obtained."

Optimism is good, but to help temper the stretch goals, what leaders sometimes want and need is a sanity check, an honest, independent reflection. West adds: "I think it's a matter of the leadership of boards thinking specifically about risk. Few do that. Most boards look at business risks, but my impression is that examination of overarching risks is relatively rare."

Outside advisers offer one avenue for unbiased perspective. Some CEOs have certain friends or peers they designate as "counterpointers," people whom they trust to tell it to them straight, and whose relevant experiences can save the executive from learning the hard way. Turning to an informed, objective resource can help center thinking and minimize surprises.

The same discipline needs to be exerted inside the organization as well. No matter how flat one's structure, CEOs are CEOs, and employees do tend to be intimidated by them. So, reports from subordinates, although not meant to mislead, often come with a gloss that can overemphasize positive news and underemphasize genuine risk conditions. For CEOs it can mean identifying, as Winston Churchill did, a separate and independent unit whose sole mission is to present them with the facts, just as they are.

Enforce a Common Risk Language and Nomenclature

There is a real need for management to more precisely define risk and develop a common terminology around uncertainty, risk assessment, and diagnosis. Current understanding often focuses on half of the definition—namely, that risk is the possibility of suffering harm or loss in the future. But in many of the recent corporate scandals, it was the failure of overseers to properly assess current risk—not future risk—that landed those companies in trouble. In these instances and others, risk discussions often fail to penetrate to the real issues of concern.

Rod Eddington, CEO of British Airways, remarks: "If you talked to people in the airline industry in the recent past, they very quickly got on to operational risk. Of course, today, we think of risk as the whole of business risk. We think about risk across the full spectrum of the things we do, not just the operational things. We think of risk in the context of business risks, whether they're risks around the systems we use, whether they're risks around fuel hedging, whether they're risks around customer service values. If you ask any senior airline person today about risk, I would hope they would move to risk in the true, broader sense of the term."

The task for boards and management is to look at these other dimensions and supply a common context and language, shared with all employees, to guide discussion. Only in this way can they be assured that both parlance and understanding are uniform across their enterprise.

ACTION ITEMS

The leaders with whom we've spoken are structuring and responding to risk in a variety of ways. This summary chapter provides an "at a glance" amalgam of their common insights and perspectives.

We live in a time of chronic uncertainty. No one person or group, no matter how specialized or well-trained, will reasonably be able to predict or manage the full set of risks that can blanket an enterprise. Increasingly, risk management and business continuity planning will become intrinsic to a company's culture and a part of everyone's responsibility. In this way, companies will breed an environment in which employee and key stakeholder confidence can grow and remain strong. As noted risk thinker Felix Kloman states: "We can never know the future. We can only prepare for it more intelligently."

Intelligent Preparedness

The common view among those with whom we've spoken is that risk must be managed at the center of the organization, otherwise the company's risk orientation will be indistinct, its approach rudderless. Ultimate oversight responsibility should rest with the board of directors. Functional responsibility, in most cases, belongs to the chief risk officer or other equivalent, independent C-level or senior VP figure empowered with the necessary authority. Surfacing, assessing, and responding to risks falls on many shoulders. There are a number of ways to coordinate the process. By way of one example, internal audit can act as the central command unit for a company's strategic risk management activities, leveraging and serving the communication needs of the board, the CEO, and the risk management function to whom it reports.

In addition, perspective and third-party objectivity should be actively sought on two fronts. First, key stakeholders—investors, lenders, vendors, customers, and employees (and sometimes the surrounding community)— should be engaged in regular and meaningful two-way communication to share news and views on existing and emerging risks, solicit feedback, and address opportunities and concerns. This area is frequently overlooked at present, but is likely to gain increasing traction. Second, external auditors, in addition to the role required of them by securities regulations, should be expected and enlisted to provide frequent and timely observations to management and the audit committee on the company's risk profile, the adequacy of controls, and the effectiveness of risk responses as these come to their attention.

By tightly aligning and linking these functions, activities, people, and skill sets, companies can work to cultivate a nimble and sustainable approach to managing risk.

RECOMMENDATIONS

1. Empower the board with ultimate risk oversight responsibility.

2. Consider a separate strategic risk committee to handle business risk while charging the audit committee with financial risk.

3. Assign functional risk management responsibility to a senior management officer.

4. Seek objective, 3rd party feedback on risk concerns from stakeholders and outside advisors.

Governance

Today, boards must oversee not only compliance, but also performance. This marks a shift. Good boards have always been diligent in their review of legal, regulatory, and ethical standards. But now the best boards are looking beyond traditional conformance duties to something more active. As part of their oversight responsibility they are taking steps to identify and understand stakeholder expectations. They do this recognizing that the processes that guide strong stewardship have an impact on such intangible drivers as reputation and brand, which in turn have a direct effect on the company's ability to generate long-term financial value. All of this has an impact on the risk, and ultimately the reward, borne by the company.

The table below lists questions good boards are adding to their governance agenda.

The Governance Agenda: *To What Extent Do Stakeholders Expect Boards To . . .*	
BOARD OPERATIONS	• Include a balance of executive and non-executive directors—offering a mix of financial, business, and personal skills appropriate to the needs of the organization—who have the time and energy necessary to meet their growing responsibilities?
	• Have the independent directors meet informally without the CEO or other non-independent directors?
	• Have access to appropriate training and independent professional advice on issues members deem necessary?

(continued on next page)

The Governance Agenda *(continued)*

STRATEGY	• Participate actively in strategy development? • Review and challenge the strategy? • Create a strategically adaptable organization that responds quickly to changing market opportunities?
CORPORATE CULTURE	• Foster openness with management? • Support management's organizational code of conduct? • Promote the use of appropriate incentives that make such codes meaningful?
MONITORING AND EVALUATION	• Ensure that the organization complies with all relevant laws and regulations, and with accounting, human resource, and other internal policies? • Understand organizational risks and be informed routinely about how they are managed? • Apply a rigorous process for evaluating the performance of the CEO?
STEWARDSHIP	• Uphold rigorous standards for individual member's preparedness, participation, and candor? • Protect the organization and its stakeholders from the potential damage of conflicts of interest? • Safeguard stakeholder interests, in part by ensuring that communication with various stakeholders is thorough, timely, and transparent?

Source: *A New Focus on Government, KPMG, 2002*

Strategic Risk
Management

As a topic, strategic or enterprise risk management has received a fair amount of attention and is recommended by many practitioners, consultants, and others—including ourselves—as the most cohesive model for risk management. Behind the name, though, strategic risk management is really just plain, good risk management practice suited up. The reason for its buzz has less to do with any bold breakthrough in thinking than with the continuing growth and evolution of risk management as a profession, along with discipline, structure, and rigor in application.

Risk management didn't arrive on the scene as a holistic practice. Rather, it lapped up on our shores in waves. The financial services and insurance industries swept in one sense of it, the IT community another, and health and safety groups others still. Each had its own language and agenda. Only in more recent times has it become clear that we're all talking about the same philosophical principles.

For modern companies, the challenge is to make a similar evolution within their own walls. Pattie Dunn, vice chairman of Barclays Global Investors and a member of the board of Hewlett-Packard, says: "I think what boards tend to miss and what management tends to overlook is the need to address risk holistically. They overlook the areas that connect the dots because risk is defined so atomistically and we don't have the perspective and the instrument panel that allows us to see risk in a 360 degree way."

A Strategic Risk Management Model

Peter Oppenheimer of Apple calls risk: "The degree to which an outcome varies from expectation." Regardless of the specific nature of individual risks, risk management consists of two functions: risk assessment and risk response. This is strategic risk management at its most fundamental.

Once the core business imperatives have been outlined, the task of risk analysis is to identify, weigh, and prioritize the possibility of unexpected events and their consequences on a company's strategy, image, and stakeholder value, as well as to continuously monitor and measure performance and foster regular and sincere two-way communication with stakeholders. The task of risk response activities is to map how best to mitigate or optimize those risks, understand the effectiveness of current responses and related controls, and develop new ones where needed.

Both the business risk ownership and categories model and the strategic risk management model, shown below, present some recommended considerations.

Strategic Risk Management Agenda

The task for boards, of course, is to ensure the effectiveness of their risk model. With that in mind, here are some action items for the strategic risk management agenda for boards and CEOs to consider:

☐ Appoint a C-level risk leader, empowered not only with the responsibility, but the authority, to act on all risk management matters.

BUSINESS RISK OWNERSHIP AND CATEGORIES MODEL

BUSINESS RISK OWNERSHIP

Board
Ultimate Risk Oversight Responsibility

Management	CEO	Board	Audit Committee	CRO	Internal Audit

Responsible for Setting Tone-at-the-Top

RISK CATEGORIES

External

Shareholders
- Financial returns
- Accurate and timely disclosure
- Quality of leadership/ intellectual capital

Customers
- Product Safety
- Customer service
- Responsible marketing practices

Suppliers/Partners
- General terms and conditions
- R&D partnerships
- Contingencies

Competitors
- Market share
- R&D investment

Financial

Credit
- Liquidity
- Cash management
- Collections

Market
- Interest rate
- Foreign exchange
- Commodity prices

Structure
- Debt
- Equity

Reporting
- SEC filings
- Accurate and timely disclosure
- Earnings guidance
- Control systems

Operational

Process
- New product development
- Sales and marketing
- Control and documentation
- Support structure

HR
- Employees
- Appropriate training
- Risk culture

Physical plant
- Security
- Property
- Leaseholds
- Equipment

Strategic

Governance
- Integrity
- Accountability
- Reputation
- Independence
- Adequacy of oversight
- Adequacy of risk structure

Business model
- Market dynamics
- Mergers/acquisitions
- Risk concentrations
- Competitors

Planning
- Benchmarking
- Testing
- Exit strategy

External relations
- Investors
- Partners
- Customers
- Community

Regulatory

Financial
- Sarbanes-Oxley
- Officer certifications
- Internal Control over financial reporting

Labor
- OSHA
- ADA
- Foreign labor certification

Environmental
- Emissions
- Pollutants

Policy
- Legislation
- Lobbying

Information

Intellectual property
- Intangible assets
- Inventorying and reporting
- Protecting

Decision support
- Systems
- Data mining
- Standardization
- Global consistency

Information technology
- Networks
- Hardware
- Software
- Intranets

STRATEGIC RISK MANAGEMENT MODEL

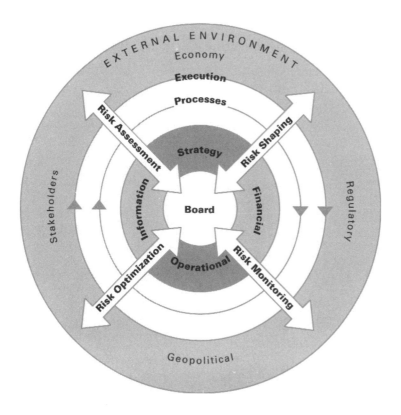

☐ Ensure that this leader is independent and can objectively work with the company's internal risk management function (internal audit), the company's external advisers (external audit, legal, etc.), and the governing decision maker and oversight function (the CEO and board).

☐ Satisfy yourselves with the depth of current risk analysis and the range of responses, both from a mitigation and optimization standpoint.

☐ Assure yourselves that the risk information they receive is accurate, clear, and relevant.

☐ Actively require and participate in regular dialogue with key stakeholders.

☐ Strive to build a culture where risk management and strategic planning are interlinked.

TRANSFORMING COMPLIANCE INTO ACTIVE SUPPORT

Internal Audit: More than Just Numbers

Many of the leaders we spoke with are elevating the internal audit function to the core "intelligence" unit of their risk management operations. Breaking out of the historic, compliance only tradition, these remolded internal audit departments are working to fill the enterprise risk management space and are taking an active leadership role in risk assessment and management. By effectively serving as the eyes and ears of the organization, they are conducting continuous quality initiatives, benchmarking, and identifying ways to improve operations and profit. In this way, internal audit can better distill the key information management needs to anticipate and react to changing market conditions.

As internal audit functions evolve to meet senior executive and board expectations, the center of gravity will increasingly become the management of strategic risk. Traditional internal audit responsibilities will be recalibrated to integrate a risk versus compliance-only focus into each aspect of the function, the underpinnings for which will be identifying and prioritizing specific operational and financial risks, helping define the levels of risk the organization is willing to accept, and developing the range of experience needed to monitor, measure, and manage those risks effectively.

In some cases, to achieve these aims management will need to expand its internal audit team beyond number crunchers. This will involve including other individuals skilled in areas critical to the organization's success, such as IT, procurement, and supply-chain management. They will also need to make sure the team features members who have a seasoned understanding of the types of risks and issues facing the business—not just domestically, but overseas as well, depending on the company's foreign operations exposure— and to ensure that internal audit planning takes into consideration external business drivers and industry trends. The needs and concerns of the company's key customers should also be reflected.

Realizing this evolved view of the internal audit function will involve board and management agreement on a number of key points. The agenda questions they must discuss center on a redefined view of the internal audit mission.

Internal Audit Agenda: *Are Board and Management Satisfied that the IA Functions . . .*
• Have been given a clear mandate to help manage the critical business risks and exposures that determine the organization's success or failure?
• Exhibit a detailed understanding of these key business risks and know how they enable or impede the organization in building shareholder value?
• Continually and appropriately assess the effectiveness of risk responses?
• Proactively communicate with management and the board?
• Competently analyze business risk and work effectively with all units or divisions to develop appropriate risk responses?
• Potentially contribute to operational and financial performance improvement?
• Have the necessary complement of skills to carry out their duties and meet these elevated requirements, or, if not, have considered whether outsourcing or cosourcing could improve the cost/benefit ratio/expertise required?

The External Audit:
More than Just a Required Relationship

The audit process yields a great deal of valuable information about continuous and knowledgeable risk insights. It too has evolved into a more meaningful function over time.

The traditional audit was developed in the industrial age, a time when financial statements captured a company's most strategic components: the physical capital of property, plant, and equipment. Today's audit is far more comprehensive. Rather than diving into the filing cabinets to tick and tie the paper trail, today's external audits start with a proper understanding of the business and the competitive environment in which a company operates. What sets today's audit apart is the recognition that business processes are dynamic and subject to a number of influencing factors.

Legislation such as the Sarbanes-Oxley Act of 2002—the landmark legislation affecting corporate governance, financial disclosure, and the practice of public accounting—and other regulations are adding new or different responsibilities for both the company and the auditor.

The chart below presents a sampling of some business risk considerations that the external auditor may consider with regard to the audit process, including discussions with management and the audit committee.

The External Audit Agenda:
What Your External Auditor May Do Regarding Risks
STRATEGIC ANALYSIS • Identify critical elements of the business environment that may impact financial reporting and the audit strategy—elements that include competition, technology, economic conditions, legislation, and industry issues. How are business strategy, products and services, customers, industry issues and critical drivers of success defined?
BUSINESS PROCESS ANALYSIS • Acquire an in-depth understanding of the business processes supporting the strategy in order to obtain a more detailed understanding of how the business operates and to determine what criteria or measurements are used to gauge company performance against objectives. Consider the key business activities and the controls associated with them.

(continued on next page)

The External Audit Agenda *(continued)*

RISK IDENTIFICATION AND ASSESSMENT

• Once critical strategies and supporting processes are understood and mapped, the auditor should interact with members of management to elucidate the primary risks that could threaten attainment of the business goals. The auditor will consider how management is addressing and controlling risks in developing their audit strategy and plan.

BUSINESS MEASUREMENT

• Focus on the processes and variables that have the greatest impact on the financial results. These processes could consist of product, customer service, credit delivery, or others. These measurements may be compared to financial risks, benchmark data, or other appropriate measures to see what gaps are revealed.

SUBSTANTIVE AUDIT PROCEDURES

• Perform substantive audit procedures to obtain audit evidence as to whether the assertions in the financial statements that relate to certain identified risks are free of material misstatement. As part of performing these procedures, the auditor may obtain direct or indirect evidence about management's responses to identified risks.

CONTINUOUS IMPROVEMENT

• The best audits are continuous processes with the above steps taken in an integrated, as opposed to a sequential, order.

BUSINESS RISK PROFILE

• The auditor may consider preparing a detailed business risk profile to clarify conditions or activities that relate to the company's business plans and to document the external and internal forces that might affect both those plans as well as the financial statements.

Maximizing Shareholder Value
Within Acceptable Risk Tolerances

The traditional emphasis with regard to risk management has been defensive: how best to protect one's rearguard. This is changing. The reward side of the equation is finally getting attention. With this exposure, more of us accept that risk eradication is not the only option. Just as an investor can tweak his portfolio in line with changing risk tolerances, corporate risk managers and boards can do the same. Increasingly, their goal is one of maximizing the return achievable for the level of risk the organization is willing to take.

For management, this may mean reducing excessive risk mitigation strategies on those risks that analysis has deemed less material, thereby saving costs. For instance, a company may decide that the cost of ensuring a given asset is too high relative to the probability or replacement cost of loss, and to slacken its insurance coverage on that asset accordingly. In other cases it could permit greater risk taking where tolerances are shown to be greater. Thus, an experienced, well-established, and disciplined trading unit may be granted higher trading limits than a newer or less well-established unit.

While optimization can allow for some complicated footwork, for it to be effective, management should ensure that:

☐ Risk limits are understood and communicated.

☐ Risk tolerances are weighted and shared appropriately across the enterprise so the monetary consequences of high-risk activities are balanced against an appropriate number of stable or low-risk activities.

☐ Discrete or decentralized business unit risks are considered in the aggregate to gauge whether or not they exceed the entity's risk appetite as a whole.

☐ Risk balancing and optimization is an iterative and continuous process.

☐ Due consideration is given to the impact an optimization decision made in one area of the organization might have on other material risks.

The boards and executives with whom we've spoken are investing time in understanding the techniques that are available and make the most sense for their business. Many are including a study of the three types of approaches described in the following management agenda.

Optimization Agenda:
Techniques for Boards and Management

RISK SPREADING

Concentration risk, be it in an area of innovation, or in a specific geography or product, can expose a company to great risk if the innovation doesn't work, the geography becomes unstable or the product becomes passé. By monitoring its concentration risk, a company ensures greater operating flexibility and gives itself the option to increase or pull back from the investment as circumstances warrant. For some R&D innovations, this can help a company defer its final decision on a project until the outcome is more certain. Risk spreading alters the cost/benefit ratio of withdrawing from a given project and permits a company to share its risk across multiple activities.

SCENARIO BUILDING

Other optimization approaches take a capital-markets perspective, using scenario building to test the relationship between a given set of risk variables and their projected impact on the stock price and public markets. For example, in the post-Sarbanes-Oxley market environment, where complicated financial deals may be viewed with suspi-

(continued on next page)

Optimization Agenda *(continued)*

> cion, it is prudent for company management to factor economic, financial, and perception considerations in their merger or acquisition calculations. In this way, risk itself becomes much more tightly interwoven in the strategic, business, and capital planning process.
>
> FINANCIAL RESTRUCTURING
>
> The least high-tech and often ignored avenue for optimizing reward is by lowering a company's cost of capital. Our current "back-to-basics" business management mentality is encouraging a sensible cash consciousness. By improving cash flow, reducing debt and costs, company executives will lower their beta or volatility risk, and contribute directly and positively to the bottom line through improved consistency.

CONCLUSION

Trying to enclose risk is a bit like trying to embrace water: It has a habit of seeping into just about everything. The pervasiveness can seem daunting. Yet most risks can be channeled and directed in less threatening ways. Those that pose little hazard can be mopped up and disposed. Those that present a more serious danger can be dammed up and contained. And others, with thought and ingenuity, can be captured and transformed into new sources of value.

Knowing the best way to respond requires a process for understanding, anticipating, and planning for risk. It requires effective risk management—a method of formalizing the intuitive and for seeing, as was said of our second president, John Adams, large things largely.

The CEO and the board of directors can use this concluding high-level checklist to assist with risk identification and assessment:

A Checklist for Identifying and Assessing Risk

ESTABLISH A PROCESS	• What is the organization's tolerance for risk?
	• What is the common risk language and nomenclature?
	• What is the process for analyzing and responding to risk?
	• Who is responsible for risk management? What is the support structure?
	• Do you have the right people with the needed training and experience?
STRATEGIC RISK	• Are the critical strategies appropriate to enable the organization to meet its business objectives?
	• What are the risks inherent in those strategies, and how might the organization identify, quantify, and manage these risks?
	• How much risk is the organization willing to take?
	• What risks result from e-business developments?
OPERATIONAL RISK	• What are the risks inherent in the processes that have been chosen to implement the strategies?
	• How does the organization identify, quantify, and manage these risks given its appetite for risk? How does it adapt its activities as strategies and processes change?
FINANCIAL RISK	• Have operating processes put financial resources at undue risk?
	• Has the organization incurred unreasonable liabilities to support operating processes?

(continued on next page)

A Checklist for Identifying and Assessing Risk *(continued)*

	• Has the organization succeeded in meeting measurable business objectives?
REGULATORY RISK	• What risks are related to compliance with regulations or contractual arrangements—not just those that are financially based?
	• Have all areas of regulatory risk been considered: SEC, securities exchanges, IRS, industry regulators, Department of Labor, other state/Federal/foreign regulators?
INFORMATION RISK	• Is our data/information/knowledge reliable, relevant, and timely?
	• Are our information systems reliable and secure?
	• Do our security systems reflect our e-business strategy?
EXTERNAL RISK	• What risks have yet to develop? These might include risks from: new competitors or emerging business models, recession, relationship, outsourcing, supply chain, regulatory, political or criminal, financial disasters (rogue traders), and other crisis and disaster risks.
	• What are the risks to brand and reputation inherent in how the organization responds to events or executes its strategies?

Source: *Understanding Enterprise Risk Management, KPMG, 2000*

CHAPTER 2

The Salt Lake Olympics and Risk's Shifting Sands

"Why shouldn't truth be stranger than fiction.
Fiction, after all, has to make sense."

—Mark Twain

"Felix. Hey. Check this out," said Ze'ev, calling from about 50 yards away.

Unger sidestepped, through the snow, down to where Yerushalmi was standing and gesturing. With only two days to go before the opening ceremonies, John "Felix" Unger was checking out the "hot spots" in the security plan.

"Here, look at this," said Ze'ev Yerushalmi. "A guy standing here could pick off the skiers as they come off the jump."

Unger raised the binoculars up to his eyes and looked through the lenses. Sure enough, he had an unimpeded view of the slope where ski jumpers would land after exiting the ramp. Even with security people around the periphery of the woods, somebody waiting here would be out of sight, with a clear opportunity to do damage. Felix was glad the plan had included troopers patrolling well inside the woods. Even so, the team had the daunting task of securing 22 key Winter Olympic sites covering 900 square miles of territory.

Felix, nicknamed at age 12 for Jack Lemmon's character in *The Odd Couple*, was an odd coupling with Ze'ev Yerushalmi. Unger had been in the Secret Service during the first Bush administration, and for six of eight years of Clinton's. He was a strategist who was also responsible for liaison with the FBI. Whenever the President traveled, Unger was in the advance team that scoped out everywhere the President would be driven, walk, eat, and sleep.

Ze'ev Yerushalmi had been an agent with Israel's Shin Bet counterintelligence service. Unlike Unger, who had the rugged look of an athlete and the demeanor of a military officer, Yerushalmi wore thick black-rimmed glasses, was tall and thin, and looked like a computer nerd. No one would have guessed by looking at him that he was a karate black belt with extensive contacts in the intelligence services of two dozen countries, among them, many former KGB agents. Because of the fickle nature of world politics, Israel had few "official" relationships with these countries' intelligence groups, but covertly there were important channels between Shin Bet and even some operatives in Arab countries. Yerushalmi was a key player in developing many of those channels.

When Salt Lake succeeded in being named host city for the 2002 Winter Olympic Games in 1997, the U.S. embassies in Kenya and Tanzania had not yet been bombed, and neither had the USS *Cole*. Security against terrorism was on the list of priorities, and in light of the Atlanta bombing in 1996, had even moved up a couple of notches. But by the end of October 2000, with the embassy and *Cole* bombings both now history, the terrorism threat had moved close to the top of the list. The Salt Lake Olympic Committee had contracted with Unger that December, and Felix had brought in Yerushalmi in February 2001. With about a year before the Games commenced, the "odd couple" had their work cut out for them.

ASSESSING THE CHALLENGE

Unger first flew in to Salt Lake in November 2000 when he was on the "short list" of candidates for the job. Earlier, he was interviewed back in Washington, D.C., where he had been consulting. Now, he returned in early December to set up his office, rent an apartment and car, and begin thinking through the challenges he faced.

It was decided early on that Unger's position not be made public. His operation would be embedded in the activities of the committee, and he'd be identified only as a staff person. In reality, he had command of all Olympic security operations, and a big budget to pay for it. Washington had made a sizable contribution to the security budget in Atlanta, and more than doubled it for Salt Lake. In Washington's view, U.S.-hosted Olympic Games constituted a national event, and thus the federal government shared in the security responsibilities.

It took Unger two days after he arrived to find an apartment and car, set up a checking account, and arrange for an unlisted telephone at his apartment. For the next two weeks, he visited the various designated Olympic sites. He had a microcassette recorder, and at each venue he recorded terse observations that he would transcribe later. He wanted to avoid carrying a clipboard and taking notes, and instead remain inconspicuous to workers or any others who might be at each location.

As he used to do when he was in the Secret Service, Unger tried to get inside the head of an assailant. The objective with an assassin is to kill the President—pure and simple. The assassin is not concerned about publicity, or scaring people, just killing one person. A terrorist, on the other hand, is primarily interested in publicity. The idea is to do something big, loud, and destructive. Victims are the secondary targets; the media is the primary.

With upward of two million Olympic attendees, often crowded into a dozen separate locations, there was certainly opportunity for mayhem. And there was no shortage of motives in the world of 2001. The key would be to deprive the terrorists of the means for wreaking havoc. Unger preferred securing an enclosed space, like an arena. You could establish an outer security perimeter, use metal detectors to check everyone going in, have a second area for checking photo IDs, and significantly lower the odds of incidents.

Where a venue lacked a physical enclosure, such as a building, you had to create a virtual enclosure, using portable barriers. Again, the intent was to limit entry only to those who passed through metal detector and ID checkpoints. But in this case, you could not lower the odds as much as in a building or arena,

The various Olympic sites were a mixed bag. Outdoor venues mitigated the effectiveness of an airborne biological agent, or a conventional bomb. In the first instance, the chemical would disperse quickly, and in the second, there would be no physical structure collapse to compound the number of injuries and deaths. But there was also no physical barrier to prevent someone from shooting into the crowd from outside. One thing Unger knew for sure—to some extent, every venue was "in play."

OLD DOGS AND NEW TRICKS

By the time Yerushalmi came on board, Unger had been looking over the Olympic Games sites for seven weeks, identifying apparent "security holes" and thinking about how he'd carry out an attack. He wondered how much of what he'd learned was applicable to the new challenges he faced.

In preparation for trips by the President, Unger and the Secret Service tried to leave no stone unturned. Their work depended on a lot of intelligence gathering, and cataloging the names and photos of people in the local areas covered by the itinerary. Prime prospects' names and photos would be distributed to all Secret Service agents and local law enforcement. Some prospects would be put under surveillance that would begin days before the President's trip.

In addition to intelligence gathering, the Secret Service made sure that motorcade schedules and routes were not announced—a result of the Kennedy assassination—and that virtually every foot of the path the President would walk, from parked automobile to rostrum, was inspected with a view to preventing any opportunity for those with malicious intent.

As Unger knew, mistakes were an opportunity to learn, and the Secret Service had made several since 1963. After Kennedy's death, the Secret Service made some sweeping process changes. The assassinations of Martin Luther King and Robert Kennedy in 1968 served as case studies. As a result, both Johnson and Nixon, from the perspective of assassination attempts, had relatively uneventful presidencies.

Then the paths of Gerald Ford and Lynette "Squeaky" Fromme crossed in Sacramento on September 5, 1975. She tried to shoot the President. And, only 17 days later, Sara Jane Moore fired a shot at Ford in San Francisco. Again, there were process changes, and for six years the Secret Service prevailed. But on March 30, 1981, John Hinckley Jr. emptied a six-shot revolver, hitting President Reagan, his press secretary, James Brady, Secret Service agent Timothy McCarthy, and Metropolitan Police Officer Thomas Delahanty. Once more, new procedures were put in place.

As for terrorist attacks, in 1995 there was the Oklahoma City bombing. But that was the work of domestic terrorists, and there had been no foreign strikes in the United States. And in February 2001 there were no U.S. government organizations doing concerted case studies of terrorist acts.

American facilities in other countries, such as the embassies in Africa and the USS *Cole* in Yemen, had been attacked, and intelligence channels were buzzing with rumors about a big event somewhere within the contiguous 48 states. But solid information about where or when was missing.

The Salt Lake Winter Games of 2002 was a tempting terrorist target, and it wouldn't be the first time the Olympics was selected for terrorist action: In 1972 terrorists had struck in Munich, knowing, as with previous Olympics, there would be worldwide television coverage of the event. The 2002 Games would be held on U.S. soil, and authorities expected a huge influx of visitors from other countries. As a result, in February 2001, Unger would be the first person whose job would be to explicitly protect a national event in a U.S. city from terrorists and terrorist attacks. And as he awaited the arrival of Ze'ev Yerushalmi, he was beginning to feel overwhelmed.

PLANNING A PLAN

Unger had first met Yerushalmi in March 1993 while doing some advance work on former President George Bush's trip to Kuwait scheduled for one month later. Yerushalmi had gotten wind of an assassination plot involving Iraqi nationals and passed the information on to the Secret Service through Unger. The American was surprised at how well "connected" this gangly Shin Bet "spook" was.

After having foiled the assassination attempt and spearheading the arrest of those involved, Unger had arranged to meet Ze'ev in Geneva in July 1993. Over a dinner that lasted five hours, the two men shared war stories and forged a relationship based on mutual respect and twinges of sincere admiration.

They were to work together again soon afterward, in preparation for the historic signing of the Oslo Agreement by Yitzhak Rabin and Yasir Arafat on the White House lawn on September 13, 1993. Unger, in charge of security for that event, was in constant touch with Yerushalmi about any rumblings of plans to disrupt the signing. Yerushalmi's sources at that time were well placed within several Palestinian opposition groups, Hezbollah in Lebanon and in the Libyan government in Tripoli.

Despite the high levels of security routinely in place at the White House, Unger was taking no chances. "Do I have anything to worry about, Ze'ev?" he asked.

"Yes. If Rabin doesn't have enough sugar in his coffee, he may not smile for the cameras," chuckled the Israeli.

The event went smoothly, and despite his obvious reluctance, Rabin did shake Arafat's hand. Now, almost eight years later, Unger and Yerushalmi would be working together again. Felix, under great pressure to get the ball rolling as quickly as possible, felt that Ze'ev provided complementary skills and insights to his own. He wanted to make sure that whatever the two men came up with was fully deployed and tested at least one month before the Games began. That left him only about eleven months to conceive, build, test, and certify, so there was virtually no tolerance for false starts and stops.

Yerushalmi flew into Salt Lake from Kennedy Airport in New York. He had arrived there three days earlier on a flight from Moscow, where he'd had clandestine meetings with Russian intelligence people to swap information about Chechnya and Iran. Ze'ev had tips about planned bombings in Grozny, the major city in Russia's troublesome Chechen Republic. In return, he sought information about the secret sale of plutonium to the Iranians. The Russians had assured him that the sales were a myth.

Like Unger, Yerushalmi took just two days to get settled in at Salt Lake. On the morning of the third day, he and Unger met in Felix's apartment at 8:00 a.m. and brainstormed until 9:00 p.m. The living room was littered with maps of the United States, Utah, and the specific Olympic Game sites; large flip-chart pages pasted on walls; empty containers of Chinese food and empty bags of fast-food burgers and fries.

For the first hour or two, the pair tended to free associate. Unger read the notes he had transcribed from his visits to the various sites, and he added extemporaneous comments.

"I guess the first thing we need to decide is our primary and secondary objectives," he said, more to himself than to Yerushalmi. "We need to decide if the primary objective is containment and mitigation, or prevention."

"I think prevention has to be number one, and containment is the contingency," Ze'ev answered with conviction. "We've got to make it as difficult as possible, and raise the odds against success too high to tolerate," he added.

"Well, the Salt Lake Olympic Committee agrees," revealed Unger. "I explained to them that preventing an action is always a gamble unless you have unlimited time and resources available—and we have neither. Their answer was that I should create the best plan possible, then make it even better."

"Okay, then," Ze'ev said, "let's build the best prevention plan the world has ever seen. . . ."

Over the next three weeks, the pair put in 14-hour days, six days a week. They read through the Utah Department of Transportation's road demand assessments, which analyzed traffic volumes, flows, bottlenecks, and needs. They visited the airport after having spent a full day scrutinizing its blueprints. In addition to finding some discrepancies between the blueprints and the actual terminal buildings, they identified over 10 different ways someone could gain unauthorized access to the aircraft and cargo areas. They drove the road systems that led to the Olympic sites from all points of the compass, and took note of overpasses, bridges, points where roadways merged, and the like. If a group planned to attack the Olympics, they would need to travel to the sites and bring weapons, bombs, or chemical/biological agents. Felix and Ze'ev wanted to know, firsthand, every means of access to those sites.

After three weeks, the two were back in brainstorming mode. This time they met at Ze'ev's rented house. "There's no way we'll be able to do this alone," Unger observed. "We've got to integrate local and state police, fire, and other emergency-response groups into any plan. We'll also need close cooperation from FBI, CIA, CDC, and federal labs. The threat is not just to the Olympic sites, but also to Utah and surrounding states."

"The key will be how we cooperate," Yerushalmi pointed out. "We won't have the time to go through proper channels. We will need tight integration and coordination, and a clear mandate from the highest levels to avoid control issues. Believe me, there were many times where Mossad and Shin Bet argued about who was in charge, and bad things happened right under our noses."

The remainder of that day, and the day after, Felix and Ze'ev pulled the pieces of a plan together. It was aimed primarily at prevention but had lots of contingency elements designed to mitigate and contain any attack that eluded detection and preemptive disruption.

SELLING THE PLAN

By the second week of March 2001, Unger and Yerushalmi were ready to present the plan at a special Salt Lake Olympic Committee meeting. They hoped to get committee approval first, then use committee contacts to sell it at the state level. Meanwhile, Unger was using his own contacts to presell the plan to the federal agencies.

"Now, let me get this straight," said Joe Norda, one of the committee members, "you expect to integrate about 60 different local, state, and federal agencies, coordinated out of a building in downtown Salt Lake, and linked together by a common computer network."

"That's right," said Unger.

"And, you expect the FBI, CIA, and all these other groups to cooperate fully and hook up to that network?" Norda continued.

"We do," said Unger.

"Is there a precedent for that?" asked Norda.

"Not yet," Unger replied, "but there's also no precedent for the level of threat we're facing. I believe we can sell this plan, but we're going to need the committee's help at the state level. I'm already pulling some strings in Washington."

The meeting lasted three hours and 35 minutes. Different committee members asked detailed questions about various aspects of the plan. But there was a consensus to approve it, and commitments to help get support from the governor, state police, local and state hospitals, and emergency medical services.

Unger had less resistance than he anticipated at the federal level. The FBI and CIA both insisted that before linking up with Unger's network, stringent firewall procedures be put in place to prevent inadvertent or purposeful intrusions into their own networks. Unger agreed.

By May about 60 organizations had formally signed on to the plan. In anticipation, Unger had contracted with a Texas-based firm to design, test, deploy, and maintain the plan's network "nerve center."

THE PLAN TAKES SHAPE

There were two critical elements to the security plan. The first involved near-real-time communications links coupled with rapid response. The second involved daily risk reassessments based on volumes of information coming in from domestic and international intelligence sources.

Had this been 1992 or even 1996, the first element—instant communication and rapid response—would have been impossible to implement. Computer networking, such as it was, could not have provided the fast, secure, wired information pathways, and wireless networking was still in gestation. But in 2001 there was high-speed, wide-band networking over existing phone lines, virtual-private networking technologies that made data secure, and wireless network access that could cover the entire 900 square miles of Olympic territory.

As for combing through volumes of incoming data and forcing critical information quickly to the top, there were software technologies designed for doing just that. They would speed through the message texts looking for key words, and prioritize the messages.

In addition to these two key plan elements, one of Unger's senior assistants had been rapidly researching existing technologies and systems designed to detect chemical or biological agents in ambient air. She was also looking into the latest systems for detecting plastic explosive in containers and luggage, and for nitrogen-based bombs in vehicles.

Months before the event, the U.S. Department of Energy had engaged the Lawrence Livermore National Labs to develop a biological detection system in time for the Games. Before that, there was no existing system for broad-scale civilian use in biological environment detection and monitoring. Starting with understanding the threat and users' needs, the lab devised a system solution, using advanced technologies, and helped test and certify both components and systems. The pace of development was astounding, given the short window and the need for high degrees of efficacy. There were extensive, direct interactions with the participating agencies and technology developers, from the concept stage through implementation, training, and operation.

Probably the most innovative plan feature was the daily assessment of risk profiles and venue hot spots coupled with dynamic deployment of security personnel. On any given day, crowd sizes would vary at different venues and different times. The security team knew that any terrorist group would want to increase the potential for death and injury. Therefore, on any given day, different venues had a higher likelihood of attack. One of Unger's contractors developed a computer program that created those risk profiles based on schedules, the popularity of events, venue capacities, times of day, and the effective depth of perimeter security. In addition, the program cranked in the profiles of various terrorist organizations, their attack preferences, and daily incoming data on known members who had recently entered the United States or bordering countries.

To Unger, the process was just like playing chess—blindfolded. In chess, you see your opponent's move and try to anticipate the next few moves. Then you try to counter the strategy with a move of your own. In this game of blindfold chess, you had to anticipate a move but you either never saw it or found out about it several moves later. So you ended up thinking, "They've made this move, even if I can't detect it. Therefore, I will make this countermove." In the end, Unger knew, it was possible that these moves could have deterred attacks, but that no one aside of the terrorists themselves would know for sure. He could live with that, preferring the security be perceived as overkill rather than inadequate. If he and his rapidly growing team could make it from two weeks before the event to two weeks after the closing ceremonies with no terrorist incidents, he would feel he'd succeeded "in spades."

IMPLEMENTING THE PLAN

By several measures, the collaborative state and federal efforts during the Salt Lake Olympics ranks as the single largest security operation in American history. In the end, over 16,000 federal agents, police, military personnel, and Olympic security guards would be assigned to the games—enough to surround each athlete with six bodyguards. Fearing that non-Olympic Salt Lake venues were also at risk, U.S. Attorney General John Ashcroft saw to it that 50 more agents were assigned to help secure such areas.

The control center for the security operation was a nondescript brick building on a Salt Lake side street. Inside a white, painted room with walls covered with maps and desks littered with computer monitors, 60 different agencies—from the FBI to the local fire department—were cooperating to try and stay at least one step ahead of terrorist threats. In the process, they would cover 20 separate venues distributed over 900 square miles as different as alpine mountainsides and outdoor entertainment stages.

Snipers, ski patrollers, helicopter-borne officers, and hazardous materials teams covered these areas under direction of specialists in the command-and-control center. No one could enter any venue without first stepping through metal detectors. And in the event of some kind of poison or biological attack, the security group had already stockpiled antidotes and antibiotics.

Elsewhere in Salt Lake, local businesses and police were adding their own efforts to security preparation. The famous Mormon Temple's gates were locked, and every entrance to the two-block Temple Square area was equipped with metal detectors. The Salt Lake airport was subjecting luggage to as many as four different checks involving bomb-sniffing canines, electronic scanning, and hand searching. And the airport would be closed during both the opening and closing ceremonies.

Not all security measures, though, were conspicuous. Unobtrusive sensors were sampling the air for the presence of chemical or biological agents. Forest Service personnel were deployed deep in the wooded areas around mountain venues, but out of sight of attendees. And hundreds of 24/7 surveillance cameras "watched" virtually all areas of the Olympic Games sites.

The numerous agencies working shoulder-to-shoulder in the security control center depended upon international cooperation and intelligence to keep hourly tabs on rumors, alerts, and reports circulating worldwide, starting weeks before the event and continuing through the closing ceremonies and for days beyond. Each day, security experts would rank the risks, and people down the chain of command would be briefed on what to look for, in particular, at various events and venues.

Security risk challenges the limits of risk assessment. The best assessments are based on good models and good intelligence. Without one or the other, you may as well simply flip a coin.

But models and solid information are ingredients. The brew is the clear objective set at the outset with respect to cost and the degree of mitigation. Whether dealing with a security or any other risk, a clear, top-level description of the objective is necessary, one based on an understanding of the risk, technical possibilities, and acceptable outcomes.

Short of turning Salt Lake and Provo into a barbed-wire enshrouded area guarded by 100,000 security professionals, there was no way to reduce the likelihood of a terrorist incident to zero. And, even in that case, the likelihood would still be finite. The goal, as with any risk, was to embrace, mitigate, or avoid it. Salt Lake could not embrace this risk and simply operate with a business-as-usual approach. And to avoid it, the Salt Lake Olympic Committee would have had to forego hosting the Winter Games.

Through the summer of 2001 the security team implemented the plan's system elements. The network was designed to handle electric utility power failures (due to storms or sabotage), laptop computers were outfitted with wireless network interface cards, and wireless "hubs" were located strategically throughout all the Olympic venues. A local police officer working with the security team had a laptop on the passenger seat in the patrol car, powered by the cigarette lighter socket, and monitored the group's e-mail bulletin board. Similar setups were found in emergency medical vehicles, unmarked FBI cars, Utah DOT vehicles, and others.

Incoming intelligence went to the command center, where specialized software prioritized and sorted the messages. Human operators then sifted through them in priority order and relayed them to various group bulletin boards. That way, individuals were not inundated with all high-priority messages, just those specific to their roles in the security plan.

By the end of August the system implementation was essentially on plan. In some cases, various elements were ahead of plan; in other cases, some were slightly behind. Unger and Yerushalmi were going over the latest set of progress reports.

"The first full-scale test is scheduled for September 19," Felix said. "I'm expecting a bunch of loose screws to fall out when we shake the box."

"Better to have the screws fall out in September than in February," Ze'ev retorted.

The men were satisfied, for the most part, with the implementation to that point. The plan schedule called for more than a dozen comprehensive tests of the system through the end of January. By the first of February, the system was to go "live," and remain live for a week after the closing ceremonies.

But Unger had an unsettling feeling.

THE JANE'S CONFERENCE

System testing was scheduled for Wednesday, September 19, and in the preceding days the stress levels were high. On September 5, Unger got a telephone call from Fred Huber, a friend and well-connected FBI agent. "Felix," he said, "I'm going to be in Salt Lake next week, how about we grab a beer and dinner?"

"What brings you to our fair town—or shouldn't I ask?" joked Unger.

"Just a boondoggle. I'm going to that Jane's Conference on protecting special events," Huber replied. "You wanna go? I'm sure I could pull a few strings. I'm flying in on Sunday, the ninth, and the conference is on Tuesday, the 11th."

"Is it okay if we have dinner on Sunday and I let you know then?" Unger said. "Things are a little crazy here right now, and I'm not sure I can slip away on Tuesday. If I can, I will, Fred."

"No problem. I'll call you when I get in on Sunday afternoon. Where can I reach you?"

"This is my cell phone number, and I have it with me all the time, Fred."

"Great, I'll talk to you then."

That Sunday, at exactly 2:13 p.m., Huber called Unger's cell phone number. They made a date to meet at 7:00 p.m. at an innocuous but excellent Japanese restaurant.

Unger knew Huber was obsessively punctual, so he made it a point to be at the restaurant by seven. As he entered, he removed his shoes and followed the hostess to a small, private room. Huber was already seated on the carpeted floor, by the tiny table, sipping tea. "Hey, stranger," Huber greeted him. "Late as usual."

Unger glanced at his watch; it was 7:01. "I hope you saved some of that tea for me."

The dinner was excellent and the company pleasant. Unger filled Huber in on what he'd been up to, and Huber gave him a sheet of paper with the Jane's Conference particulars. The conference was officially titled, "Facility Security: Protecting Infrastructure and Special Events."

"Boy, that sounds like it's right up my alley," Unger muttered after quickly scanning the page. "How about I meet you there 15 minutes before it starts?" "I want to get a good seat, so make it a half hour, okay?" Huber replied.

"Done," said Unger.

Unger knew that the Jane's organization was widely regarded as the ultimate source for defense, aerospace, and transportation information. It was also the publisher of *Jane's Defence Weekly, Jane's Fighting Ships,* and *Jane's All the World's Aircraft.* He was looking forward to the conference, and to a brief break from the high-stress security group milieu. The conference topic was certainly relevant, so he felt less guilty about taking time away from the group. After all, he told himself, he'd been working mostly seven-day weeks since December.

But Unger never made it to that conference. That same morning, his cell phone rang around 8:00 a.m. It was Yerushalmi. Nineteen terrorists had highjacked four commercial airliners. Two of them, loaded with passengers and fuel, had been flown into the World Trade Center towers; one had crashed his plane into one side of the Pentagon; and the fourth was believed to have crashed in a field in Pennsylvania. Unger fought down a wave of nausea as Yerushalmi briefed him on what would forever be known as "9/11."

Ironically, John Powers, then chairman of Corporate Communications Resource, Inc., was quoted as saying at the conference that "contingency planning is difficult to do correctly, and hard to sell politically."

Hard to sell politically? Unger thought when he read the quote. Not anymore.

A RENEWED SENSE OF PURPOSE

That infamous Tuesday, it seemed as if everyone in the security group was going through the motions. You could see that the images of the crumbling towers indelibly were imprinted on everyone's psyche. A pair of television sets was tuned to CNN, and people kept stopping what they were doing to find out what was going on and to watching the repeated video clip of the second plane plunging into the building, followed by a soundless fireball.

By Wednesday, though, Felix sensed something had changed. He couldn't precisely put his finger on it, but it seemed there was a renewed sense of purpose within the group. Its job was to prevent another terrorist attack at an event already tainted by the Black September terrorists in 1972. But even more, its job was to show that the United States was not the weak, irresolute nation that Bin Laden claimed it was, but a country capable of defending itself against unbridled hate without turning itself into a police state.

Unger found that people worked harder, stayed longer, offered suggestions, and took responsibility. The sense that someone was just doing his or her job, and the onus was entirely on management, was barely palpable from the beginning, but now it was gone, and no rubble remained.

The first test was rescheduled for September 20, and, surprisingly, not many "screws" shook out of the box. Each subsequent test in October fared better than the one before, and the process of debugging made the system more and more refined. By December all the difficult bugs had been sorted and the remaining ones were annoyances rather than showstoppers. But even these problems were ironed out during the January tests, and the system went live on schedule.

From a week before the opening ceremonies through the 15 days of events the system and the group ran the plan by the numbers. Daily risk assessments were prepared hours before the first morning events and updated by the hour throughout the day. Security people were moved around like pieces on a chessboard, countering threats that systems and people decided needed to be countered even if solid evidence of the threat was not there. The group erred on the side of excess, with the contingency containment and mitigation teams ready to jump into action at a moment's notice.

A SIGH OF RELIEF . . .

By the morning of February 24, the Winter Olympic Games of 2002 had experienced a few internal crises but not a single security-related incident. This was the day of the closing ceremonies, and Unger knew the Rice-Eccles Olympic Stadium was a hot spot. Before it was over, Jacques Rogge, the International Olympic Committee president, would address the crowd. The mayors of Salt Lake City and Turin, Italy—the host of the 2006 Olympic Games—would do the ceremonial Olympic flag exchange. If al Qaida or some other terrorist organization was to make a strike, this was the time and the place.

As they had throughout the Games, and for months before, the security team was monitoring incoming intelligence, assessing the high-risk places and times, and deploying security people and supporting systems according to that day's profiles.

As Unger scanned through the most recent spate of intelligence postings, Yerushalmi came by and put his hand on the seated man's shoulder. "Just when you were really starting to like your job, it's nearly over," chuckled Ze'ev.

"Tell me, Ze'ev, do I have anything to worry about?" asked Felix without turning his head from the screen.

"Yes," said Yerushalmi. "If you don't put enough sugar in Rogge's coffee, he may not smile for the cameras."

. . . AND A GALA CELEBRATION

That day, most of the 2500 Olympic athletes paraded into Rice-Eccles Olympic Stadium. It was to mark the beginning of the end. It was the beginning of the closing ceremony and the end of the 2002 XIX Winter Olympic Games. Joining the athletes were 55,000 visitors in the stadium and millions of television viewers around the world.

Just 17 days before, at the opening ceremony, U.S. athletes had entered the stadium carrying the tattered flag from the World Trade Center, a somber reminder of heightened risk that needed no explanation.

Compared to the ceremonial and traditional opening of the Games, this closing ceremony was more of a party. The rock-and-roll band KISS, in full face paint and body armor, shared the spotlight with Olympic skaters Katarina Witt and Kristi Yamaguchi. Afterward, Earth, Wind and Fire and Gloria Estefan sang and tap dancers danced.

Later, skiers, skaters, bobsledders, and snowboarders watched as the mayor of Salt Lake City passed the Olympic flag to his counterpart from Turin, Italy. And IOC President Jacques Rogge said, "We were thrilled by your spirit of fair play and brotherhood. Keep this flame alight. Promote the Olympic dream in your countries. You are the true ambassadors of the Olympic values."

At the end, the athletes of the 77 nations that had come to compete came down to the stadium floor for a farewell to each other and the world. During the Games, a judging controversy in figure skating dominated the news of the first 10 days. The Russians had even threatened to walk out. But in the end terrorist acts never materialized, and Rogge thanked the security operations that had kept the Games safe. Even the traffic jams that were expected to disrupt the orderly movement of visitors from venue to venue never came to pass.

Visitors came to Salt Lake. The weather cooperated. The Wasatch earthquake fault cooperated. Personnel from the 60 different local, state, and federal agencies, as well as international law enforcement and intelligence agencies, cooperated. The organizers did a commendable job of hosting the Games and a first-class job of managing the risks. And in their success are several lessons.

A SYSTEMATIC APPROACH

John "Felix" Unger, Ze'ev Yerushalmi, and Joe Norda are fictional. Nevertheless, the security systems described in this chapter reflect those actually developed. We focused on the security risk, but the Olympic Committee had several risks to deal with. And, in almost every case, the risks had discernible interrelationships.

For example, the September 11 attacks affected security, market, financial, and reputational risks. Coming less than six months before the opening ceremony, the successful terrorist attack exposed several vulnerabilities in systems meant to deal with border entry, airport, and airline security, interagency communications, and responsiveness. As a result, the security risk spiked during the time between 9/11 and February 8, 2002.

Fear of terrorism may have contributed to market risk. Less than 90 days before the opening ceremonies, nearly 20 percent of the tickets remained unsold. That was a far higher percentage than usual.

Olympic Games are not guaranteed money makers. The Games in Montreal, for example, ended up a billion dollars in debt. Salt Lake had developed a model predicated on attendance by nearly two million attendees. It also assumed average per-diem spending. There was a slight cushion built into the Olympic financing, but there was a tangible risk that Salt Lake could end up on the short end, with taxpayers having to bear that burden.

The Olympics had already been the target of terrorism twice before. If another terrorist assault succeeded in injuring or killing athletes and/or attendees, it would add to the risk of reputational damage already being pounded by allegations of bribery.

The Salt Lake Olympic Committee identified the security risk as its biggest challenge a year before the Olympics, and the World Trade Center attacks confirmed it. The approach it took, blending technology, interagency cooperation, risk modeling, and dynamic risk reassessments, helped to prevent terrorism at the Games.

The relevance to business risk is to recognize that interrelationships of market, operational, financial, and reputational risk are both real and dynamic. Like the Salt Lake Olympic Committee, there needs to be a systematic approach to assessing, monitoring, and reassessing those risks and interrelationships in order to optimize the shareholder value at any chosen risk-appetite level.

··

CHAPTER 3

Risk in a Modern Global Business Context

"The ability to define what may happen in the future and to choose among alternatives lies at the heart of contemporary societies."

—Peter L. Bernstein, *Against the Gods*

R isk, and its mastery, is the line of demarcation that separates modern times from a time when people believed the future was the mirror of the past, or else was totally unpredictable. By "modern times," we refer not to the industrial revolution, but to the Renaissance. "All the tools we use today in risk management and in the analysis of decisions and choice, from the strict rationality of game theory to the challenges of chaos theory, stem from the developments that took place between 1654 and 1760," writes Peter Bernstein in his excellent book, *Against the Gods.*[1]

Once the wheels of probability and risk management were set in motion, they transformed the world in ways comparable to the invention of the printing press and steam engine. And that transformation continues to evolve along with the evolution of commerce and trade. Thus, we find ourselves in a global business environment that at times seems fraught with risk, and we clamor for breakthroughs that can help us see through the fog of uncertainty. But the real need may be for a shared perspective and a greater degree of risk correlation.

This chapter will look at some basic questions for executives as they factor risk into their business plans and agendas, questions that include:

☐ What's your perspective?

☐ What's at stake?

☐ What's your risk appetite?

☐ Who's managing your risk?

☐ Where are you on the risk continuum?

☐ What's your risk profile?

WHAT'S YOUR PERSPECTIVE?

We are all familiar with traditional risks, such as credit and liquidity. What about less traditional risks? "Companies are coming to the realization that quite often the risks they've traditionally been insuring are not by any means the biggest risks, that they're assuming other risks that could be much more detrimental to the firm," says George R. Keller, president and chief executive officer of Winterthur International America Insurance Co., Dallas, Texas.[2]

Reputational risk, since 2001, has become a huge nontraditional area of concern. "I seriously doubt the traditional job description for a risk manager makes that person responsible for managing reputational risk. But in my view," says one executive, "that is the largest risk on our plates today—and it affects each one of us. If you are managing any company, if you are an auditor, or a regulator, or a politician with responsibilities related to the markets, all of those have had their reputations damaged by scandals and misdeeds in Corporate America."

Seeing the complex interrelationships among risks is another new development. How do your company's risks relate to one another? What effect does currency fluctuation have on interest-rate risk, for example? How does global expansion affect operations risk, and how does it relate to market risk? What effect does an earnings restatement—accounting error risk—have on reputational risk? Even a qualitative study of before-and-after polling would show that reputations suffer in the wake of restated financials, but by how much? That degree of reputation volatility has certainly grown larger following the announcements of large restatements by AOL Time-Warner and WorldCom MCI. In early June 2003, just the disclosure that the SEC was looking into some aspects of IBM's revenue recognition caused the stock to decline even as the Dow was growing.

The perspective of the person or persons responsible for overseeing—both board members and risk managers—cannot be overlooked. A "risk seeker" guarding a "risk averse" chicken coop leaves the door open to significant differences in risk evaluations. Such a person may ease controls at exactly the time when they need to be tightened. On the other hand, a risk-averse overseer could tighten the screws well beyond a corporation's risk tolerance. In that case, the shareholders could lose because risks with which they were comfortable were avoided and bottom lines were impacted.

By looking at both the negative and positive aspects of uncertainty, a corporation can work to optimize its risk. Is risk optimization something your corporation is working toward, or is the goal a more one-sided, risk-reduction strategy? How does your corporation integrate risk into business planning? Is risk management an integral part of strategy and process change, or is it treated separately?

WHAT'S AT STAKE?

When discussions of risk centered around diminished profits due to credit defaults, system failures, currency fluctuations, and the like, risk tended to be a line item that the CEO ceremoniously owned but was often unceremoniously passed down the chain of command. Today, though, with glaring reminders of just how far the mighty can fall, risk has regained much CEO and board attention—and rightly so. After all, in the final analyses it was risk management failure that shook Enron, Tyco, WorldCom, and others to their very foundations. But lest you think that risk management failure is a new millennium affliction, read on. Here are brief histories of failed risk handling that preceded the dot-com implosion. One could argue, quite convincingly, that these and others set the stage for what was to follow.

Barings[3]

Take Barings Bank, for example. This much respected, and oldest (223 years old), UK merchant bank was sold to the Dutch bank ING for one pound sterling in March 1995.

In February 1995, Barings had over $900 million in capital, but was bankrupted when a trader accumulated over a billion dollars in trading losses. How could this happen? How could a bank with a solid history of successes miss that one of its traders had jeopardized its very existence?

The Barings trader, depicted in the movie *Rogue Trader* by Ewan McGregor, was thought to be focusing on low-risk arbitrage opportunities that would leverage price differences in similar equity derivatives on the Singapore Money Exchange (Simex) and the Osaka exchange. In reality, he was buying and selling different amounts of the contracts on the two exchanges, thereby taking much riskier positions, or buying and selling different types of contracts. He was also given control over both the trading and back-office functions, which allowed him to obfuscate much of what he was doing.

Like a gambler who tries to make up his losses by increasing his bets, this trader took even bigger risks and ran headlong into the earthquake that kicked the struts out of the Nikkei index. When the dust cleared, Barings was upside down and bankruptcy was the result. But was this simply the problem of a rogue trader who circumvented otherwise good checks and balances? Not necessarily.[4]

To begin with, Barings had had little experience in trading. For example, the arbitrage trading that was supposed to be transacted was a low-risk, low-profit trade, yet the trader was reporting huge profits. Where were these profits coming from? And why were millions of dollars being wired to Singapore when arbitrage is supposed to be a cash-neutral or slightly cash-positive exercise?

An internal auditor who had gone to Singapore recommended tighter controls over the mix of trading and back-office functions, but these were never put in place. The first hint of a problem came in February 1995 when the bank's outside auditors delayed signing off on Barings' accounts. They wanted to clarify some issues with the trader in Singapore first. Literally, within weeks, the whole scheme unraveled. An account created by the trader to hold a 20,000 pound accounting error until he could resolve it through trading ultimately wound up holding over 60,000 contracts expiring in March and June that as of February 1995 totaled losses of 59 billion yen on the Simex. By March the bank was sold to ING for a pound.[5]

As you'll read later, there were several things that could have prevented the Barings disaster, but the most significant was having a policy that prevented someone from having both trading and back-office responsibilities: Barings needed more stringent internal controls.

Cendant

In December 1997, Cendant Corporation was created by the $11 billion merger of HFS and CUC International. HFS owned hotels and real estate brokerages; CUC was a direct-marketing company. Cendant's businesses included Century

21, Coldwell Banker, and other real estate services, such as Cendant Mortgage; Rent Net, a Web site for finding apartments; and a relocation service. It also owned such franchises as Avis, Days Inn, Howard Johnson, Ramada, Super 8, and Travelodge. In addition, Cendant owned a vacation time-share exchange service, tax preparation and mutual fund companies, and consumer-service programs, including a travel agency, a shopping service, and the provision of extended warranties and credit card protection.

Within five months of its creation (April 1998) Cendant announced "accounting irregularities," pegged at $115 million, which turned out to be $300 million. Its shareholders sold off enough shares to sink its market value by over $15 billion. Its CEO watched his own personal worth drop by more than $370 million, establishing the 1998 record for CEO personal loss.

The problems had begun well before the new corporation was created. From 1995 through 1997, CUC management allegedly booked fictitious revenues to meet Wall Street's expectations.[6] According to the allegations, CUC fraudulently booked $30 million in 1995. That number grew to $87 million during 1996. And during the first three quarters of 1997 (just prior to the merger) it reached $176 million.

Each year, it was alleged, CUC management created the fictitious revenues and increased the accounts receivable. And in each fourth quarter they reversed the entries to hide the false revenues from auditors. To conceal the sleight-of-hand, they then booked revenue that should have been recognized later, and used reserves set up for other purposes.[7]

Cendant's auditors discovered additional accounting irregularities, including inappropriate depreciation of certain assets and delayed recognition of insurance claims. On April 15, 1998, Cendant announced that its initial earnings of $872 million would be lowered by $115 million. On April 16 the stock lost $15 billion in value, and the first eight of what would be well over 20 shareholder lawsuits were filed against the corporation.[8]

Fraud at CUC was apparently rampant. In retrospect, the driving forces behind it seem easy to divine. When earnings goals are emphasized, there's a risk that managers will do whatever they can to make those goals. That is why a culture that emphasizes accountability, strong internal controls, and setting the right tone-at-the-top are so critical to sound risk management.

Bausch & Lomb

Like Barings Bank, Bausch & Lomb was a venerable old company. But internal mismanagement in two key divisions caused the company to lose a billion dollars of market capitalization in late 1995, and saw its revenues revert to the levels of 1991.[9]

One of the oldest continually operating companies in the United States today, Bausch & Lomb's roots reach as far back as 1853, when John Jacob Bausch, a German immigrant, set up an optical goods shop in Rochester, New York. Needing more money to keep the business going, Bausch borrowed $60 from Henry Lomb, a good friend, and promised if the business grew, Lomb would become a full partner. The rest, as they say, is history.[10]

Early on, Bausch & Lomb manufactured innovative rubber eyeglass frames as well as a variety of optical products requiring a high degree of manufacturing precision. By 1903 the firm had been issued patents for microscopes, binoculars, and even a camera shutter based on the eye's reaction to light.

In the 1900s, Bausch & Lomb continued its technological innovation of optical products. It produced the first optical quality glass made in America, developed effective sunglasses for the military in World War I, and created the lenses used on the cameras that took the first satellite pictures of the moon.

Bausch & Lomb was also the first company to develop soft contact lenses, which helped increase to mammoth proportions the number of people trading eyeglasses for contact lenses. By the early 1990s the company had a disposable contact lens that was priced for about six months worth of wearing. Its competitor, Johnson & Johnson, however, had leapfrogged to a disposable lens priced for weekly replacement, and it was eclipsing the sales of the Bausch & Lomb offering.

As happens in many industries and businesses, Bausch & Lomb corporate management set aggressive sales goals for its contact lens division, and as the SEC later discovered, some division managers stretched the rules.[11] While concentrating on playing catch-up with Johnson & Johnson on lower price disposables, Bausch & Lomb opted to push the sales problems associated with the longer term disposables off to its distribution channel. Using incentives, credit lines, return policies, and the like, this division crossed some lines with regard to revenue recognition, and the SEC took note.[12]

The CEO of 13 years stepped down in the face of increasing shareholder distrust and consternation. Here, again, is an apparent case of senior management issuing aggressive divisional goals without the appropriate controls in place. Because of its failings, Bausch & Lomb received various penalties, including the embarrassment of the SEC inquiry and findings; earnings retractions; share price volatility; and settlement of a shareholder lawsuit. Despite sustained management efforts afterward to restructure the company—including selling off the sunglasses division in 1999—Bausch & Lomb had a difficult time recovering its earlier and consistent growth levels.

These three cases did not precipitate great changes in regulatory controls. It took Enron, Tyco, and WorldCom to stir the political hornets nest. But the buzzing that culminated in the Sarbanes-Oxley legislation is rippling through all aspects of business and risk management.

WHAT'S YOUR RISK APPETITE?

Risk appetite is not about regulatory compliance. It's about how much risk your company is able to accept, manage, and optimize effectively. Yet, risk appetite is probably one of the more poorly understood aspects of risk.

Risk appetite—or risk tolerance—is a concept first associated with people, not companies. As Dan Borge points out in *The Book of Risk*: "An institution does not actually experience the consequences of the risks that it takes. An institution merely redistributes the consequences of risk to its individual human constituents—managers, employees, shareholders, citizens, members, clients, beneficiaries, and so on."[13]

Articulating your company's risk appetite is a must because, in combination with uncertainty and volatility, it is a critical factor in determining the company's "handling" of its risks. But how do you go about making that qualification? There are questionnaires that brokerage houses use to qualify an investor's risk appetite. No single question is enough to do the job. But to whom in the corporation do you give the questionnaire? The CEO? The chairman of the board?

Mature corporations establish a history, over time, that can be examined in order to distill an apparent risk appetite. But it is no guarantee for success. Examine any Fortune 500 company and consider how its risk appetite has shifted from the '80s to the '90s to the present decade. Has Time Warner, for instance, exhibited the same risk appetite over the last two years as over the previous two years?

Since risk appetite is fundamentally a human quality, it may be helpful to look at some interesting findings described in Daniel Kahneman's and Amos Tversky's Prospect Theory research. The pair, who began collaborating in the 1960s, identified some human behavior patterns overlooked by those who believe fervently in rational decision making. One finding was that emotion often disrupts self-control, which is necessary for making rational decisions. Another was that people do not always fully understand what they're dealing with, and are prone to jump to erroneous conclusions.[14] As Bernstein describes it: "We have trouble recognizing how much information is enough and how much is too much. We pay excessive attention to low-probability events accompanied by high drama and overlook events that happen in routine fashion."[15]

Our behavior as either risk averse or risk seeking is often irrational. For example, Tversky and Kahneman did an experiment in which subjects were asked to choose between an 80 percent chance of winning $4000 and a 20 percent chance of winning nothing, versus a 100 percent chance of receiving $3000. Eight out of 10 subjects choose the certain $3000 even though the riskier choice had a higher mathematical expectation—$3200. In that instance, the majority was behaving risk aversely. But when the same group was given an 80 percent chance of losing $4000 and a 20 percent change of breaking even, versus a 100 percent chance of losing $3000, 92 percent opted for the gamble. Here, they were acting like risk seekers. It turns out the gamble put them at greater risk of losing—$3200. But there was decision asymmetry at work here. They were risk averse when dealing with gains but risk seeking when dealing with losses.

A similar asymmetry occurred when the same proposition was posed using different perspectives. In this proposition a serious disease outbreak has occurred and the subject must choose between two programs, A and B. There are 600 people taken ill. If program A is selected, 200 will be saved. If program B is selected, there is a 33 percent probability that everyone will be saved, but a 67 percent probability that no one will be saved. When posed this way, 72 percent of the subjects chose the risk-averse plan A. The second time, the group was told to choose between plan C or D. With C, 400 of the 600 will die. With D, there's a 33 percent probability that nobody will die and a 67 percent probability that 600 people will die. This is exactly the same situation expressed in mortality rather than survivor terms. And 78 percent of the subjects went for the gamble. Tversky sums it up this way: "The major driving force is loss aversion. It is not so much that people hate uncertainty—but rather, they hate losing."

What makes the work of Tversky and Kahneman so important is its implications on utility. Risk decision making is a factor of uncertainty, volatility, and utility. Since the first two factors can be deduced mathematically, they should be the same regardless of who is making the decision. It is the sense of utility, however—one's personal feeling of need or value—that becomes the point of differentiation and plays such a key role in qualifying risk tolerance.

Daniel Bernoulli, in the early 1700s, postulated that a person's level of utility was inversely proportional to how much of something they already had. In other words, a rich person was more likely to be averse to a gamble on increased wealth than someone who was less wealthy.

But research in the 1970s indicates that reference points rather than absolute levels most affect utility. For example, when subjects were told they had just won $30 and were now offered a coin toss where each would win $9 for a head or lose $9 for a tail, about 70 percent of this group, with a starting wealth of $30, took the gamble. Another group, with a starting wealth of zero was offered a coin toss where heads would win

$39 and tails would win $21, or they could choose 100 percent odds of getting $30. In this case, though the end results for both groups were identical—ending up with either $39 or $21 if they chose the gamble—only 43 percent opted for the coin. These findings were opposite those one would expect from Bernoulli's theory. The group with $30 of starting wealth was risk seeking compared with the group starting out with nothing. Bernoulli would have predicted that the decision would be based on the end amounts of $39, $30, or $21, but it appears to have been driven by the reference points of $30 and nothing.

Even the amount of information can cause behavioral change. Medical researchers David Redelmeier and Eldar Shafir studied how doctors responded to choices as the number of options increased. In the first case, the physicians were asked to choose one of two options for a 67-year-old patient in chronic pain. Option one was to prescribe a medication; option two was to refer him to orthopedics. The doctors split, with about half opting for referral to orthopedics. When given a third option—a second medicinal choice—nearly two-thirds of the group opted for referral to orthopedics!

A corporation's risk appetite is really the risk appetites of those people to whom the consequences are ultimately transferred. These include executives, managers, shareholders, and stakeholders. The preceding examples of behavior variances show that arriving at some risk-appetite quantifier is at least both art and science. As risks change and proliferate, managers in a variety of industries must work to align the types and amounts of risk to what has been defined as the organization's risk appetite. It is a "C-level" executive responsibility to define that risk appetite.

WHO'S MANAGING YOUR RISK?

The changing regulatory climate is prompting the clarification of old roles and the creation of new ones. Oversight "push back" was a rare event in some boards of directors and audit committees where both groups were closely tied to the CEO. Such close CEO relationships may have helped grease the skids during the latter half of the last economic expansion, but it also paved the way for many of the abuses that have since emerged. In response to this, some positions such as the CFO and controller have been vaulted into greater authority, and much greater scrutiny is being focused on audit committees and boards of directors.

Richard Bressler, Viacom CFO, sees changing trends in CFO behavior in response to the increased scrutiny and pressure. He observes: "Stakeholders and shareholders are rewarding people for simplicity in today's market." And although Bressler doesn't put himself in the following category, he recognizes that the pressure is such that many CFOs will "stay away from elaborate types of financial instruments," adding, "They may be doing a plain vanilla transaction when there's a better transaction out there, but they don't want to do it because of the accounting treatment." As a result, he notes, "people may make bad economic decisions that may be good accounting answers."

Scott Di Valerio, Microsoft's controller, told us: "I think the role of the controller is interesting. Our role has gained some prominence in the national and international spotlight given all the regulations and the emphasis now on controls. But I don't think the role has changed. I believe there's a higher standard or emphasis that CEOs, and even CFOs, are putting on controls, which has increased the interactions that controllers are having with them discussing the design and effectiveness of the controls environment. The controller now has the opportunity to provide a better understanding of the control environment and its impact on internal and external financial reporting throughout the organization.

In addition to an elevated finance function, some companies have taken things a step further and appointed a Chief Risk Officer (CRO), a title coined by James Lam, who gave himself the tag when first hired by Financial Guaranty Insurance Group at GE Capital. While still primarily found in financial services organizations, and in utilities and energy companies, CROs are beginning to appear in other industries too. Delta Air Lines, for example, created a CRO position reporting to the CFO in December 2001. And it wasn't a knee-jerk reaction to September 11; Delta had been considering a CRO for over a year. "As CFO, I needed someone who didn't control or own the company's risks, but who was both taking note of Delta's risk issues and who had a view on the financial implications of those risks, says Michelle Burns, Delta's CFO. As such, Delta's CRO keeps Burns up to date on all Delta risks and puts values on them. The CRO's aim, says Burns, is to achieve "increased visibility of risk across the company."[16]

In August 2001, Stephen Rietiker took over as CEO of Swiss-based Sulzer Medica, a medical devices company recently spun off from its parent. In addition to having to now stand on its own, the company was facing several U.S. lawsuits following a recall of thousands of hip and knee implants. Rietiker took two immediate steps. He hired a CFO and a CRO, and both were to be peers on the executive committee. CRO Gabor-Paul Ordo says his role was "to build a holistic view of the company's risks . . . to identify all the threats and opportunities [the company] faced, and then combine them into an integrated and company-wide approach to risk management."[17]

In general, most CROs are charged with the following responsibilities:

☐ Providing overall leadership, vision, and direction for enterprise risk management

☐ Establishing an integrated risk management framework for all aspects of risks across the organization

☐ Developing risk management policies, including the quantification of management's risk appetite through specific risk limits

☐ Implementing a set of risk metrics and reports, including losses and incidents, key risk exposures, and early warning indicators

☐ Optimizing the company's risk portfolio through business activities and risk transfer strategies

☐ Improving the company's risk management readiness through communication and training programs, risk-based performance, measurement and incentives, and other change management programs

☐ Developing the analytical systems and data management capacities to support the risk management program

Not every company sees the CRO role as a separate one. While some companies have created distinct Chief Risk Officer roles, Mark Hurd, CEO of NCR, believes that "at the end of the day, the CEO is accountable." He adds, "You can put somebody in and say 'you're the Chief Risk Officer,' but they're not the ultimate risk owner in the company. They may have the title, but as CEO, I'm the guy that's going to make the decision in the end, so I better make sure I understand the risks and put a process in place to support that responsibility."

General Barry McCaffrey is a believer in what he calls "consensual leadership with decentralized operational execution." He sees a parallel between corporate and battlefield leadership, and a potential flaw that can confound the plans of both.

In recounting a parable he once heard, he said, "You see all sorts of generals. Smart ones. Not so smart ones. Good-looking ones. Not so good-looking ones. But what is consistent about them all is that they learned to surround themselves with good people. And they listened to them." The same is true with successful companies. "Most people in senior positions," says McCaffrey, "know how to cultivate talent and listen to it. They develop it, promote it, and they compensate it." Failure to do so, he says, "can lead a company to arrogance and self-deception." Ultimately, McCaffrey adds, "you follow the leader over the cliff."

WHERE ARE YOU IN THE RISK CONTINUUM?

When asked where his company was on its risk continuum, Rod Eddington, the CEO of British Airways, remarked: "We're on a journey. Like many businesses, we used to be reactive, but I think we're much more proactive now. You have to recognize that you can never hope to foresee all the risks your business faces. But, you have to try to get ahead of the curve. And if you do, chances are you'll be much better prepared than businesses that just try to be reactive."

To some extent every business practices risk management, but there are big differences in their stages of development.

Stage One

For example, every company, by law and/or lender fiat, has a variety of insurance policies, spanning liability for accidents that happen on their premises, damage to facilities and equipment from fire, and so on. In each case they're accepting a certain loss against the possibility of a huge loss. That is basic risk management.

For some companies, that's all there is. There is no formal process in place for identifying and managing other risks. When steps are taken with regard to these other risks, they are ad hoc and typically reactive. Compared with more advanced forms of risk management, this stage is primitive. It mitigates risks identified and required by others but leaves the company exposed to the "wildness" lying in wait.

Stage Two

At a more advanced stage, risk identification and management becomes a formalized process, distributed among the company's silos and embedded to a degree in divisional business and operational planning. A C-level executive may oversee some aspects of this risk management process, but it's not written in stone.

Executive management views corporate risk as the aggregate of all the silo risks; it is primarily a bottoms-up driven approach. This process has decades of success under its belt, particularly from about 1950 through 1970. But risks have grown more complex and more interrelated in the last quarter century, and this process is not designed to deal with either very effectively. This middle-of-the-road stage of risk management treats these risks as isolated threats, and just by virtue of having identified and assessed these risks it diminishes exposure to the ravages of unforeseen deviations much more so than the more primitive approach. But because it fails to account for risk correlations, it can underestimate volatilities and result in suboptimal risk-adjusted performance.

Stage Three

This leads to the third and most sophisticated stage of risk oversight, known as strategic or enterprise risk management.

As credit, currency, and political risks metamorphosed in the wake of floating currencies and rampant globalization, it became clear that traditional risk management was leaving too much to chance. Strategic risk management is a means of coordinating, overseeing, and modeling the interrelationship of important risk factors across the scope of the business.

While still new in its development, the discipline impels an organization to integrate risk into business and operational planning, and forces alignment between corporate vision and line-of-business objectives.

The generic categories covered include:

Know your goals. When times are uncertain, you need to know where you're heading. This includes strategic vision as well as tactical objectives, both long-term and short-term.

Know your environment. Be sure you understand the world in which you operate, including political, economic, social, technical, regulatory, and legal factors that might affect you.

Know yourself. Assess your organizational culture, identify your strengths and weaknesses, and determine your risk appetite and thresholds. They have a significant influence on your response to uncertainty.

Know your options. Uncertainty always creates alternatives. Conduct a strategic opportunity review to identify possible ways ahead, select your preferred route, then develop fallback and contingency plans to keep you on track. Apple's senior vice president of finance, Peter Oppenheimer, says: "Companies should take risks they have the core competencies and skills to manage and have clearly thought through, including an exit strategy, and that are strategically aligned with the business."

Know what you know. Perform a knowledge audit to define the intellectual capital in the organization, ensuring that lessons are identified and learned from previous experience.

Know what you don't know. Scope the uncertainty to define areas of maximum risk, then assess and prioritize both threats and opportunities.[18]

WHAT'S YOUR RISK PROFILE?

Over time, sometimes very brief periods, the risks, probabilities, and exposures impacting a company change. And so should its risk profile.

It is reasonable to assume that similar companies in the same industry will have similar risk profiles, but that is true only for risk description. Probabilities and severities can be significantly different.

For example, two companies that make integrated circuits would both have business risks associated with production. If one company had its own fabrication facilities while the other relied entirely on third-party production, the probabilities and severities of production risks would be far different. Clearly, the first company has more control over production than the second company. On the other hand, the second company has less risk of loss due to overcapacity. There are high overhead costs associated with fabrication facilities to which the first company is fully exposed. Company number two has essentially no risks associated with its own overcapacity (it has no fabrication facilities) and has positive opportunities associated with third-party overcapacity (e.g., lower pricing).

These differences in risk profile account for the difference between such industry peers as Coca-Cola and PepsiCo. Although the list of risks is similar, the other parameters are different. This often leads to significant differences in exposure and stakeholder returns.

According to David McNamee, president of Mc2 Management Consulting, many organizations fail to factor in the time continuum in risk profiling and risk management: "Managers often spend so much time dealing with the significant risks in the present that they find it difficult to deal with risk in a longer time horizon."[19] McNamee's position is that by focusing on the short-term risks, our approaches and controls are skewed toward mitigation. "In the short run, negative risk overwhelmed anything we could do to take advantage of short-term opportunities," he explains. But if risk planning encompasses longer planning horizons, "we have greater potential to take advantage of opportunities."

Sharalyn Preston, at KPMG, uses three dimensions to help plot risk profiles and action steps.[20] Risks are plotted against the usual probability/impact magnitude axes, and an area representing the risk appetite is drawn. From this perspective it is easy to visualize the risk management latitude one has without exceeding risk tolerance. On average, by moving toward the risk-appetite area from either side (as shown), one can optimize the risk "portfolio" for better risk-adjusted performance while remaining true to corporate risk appetite.

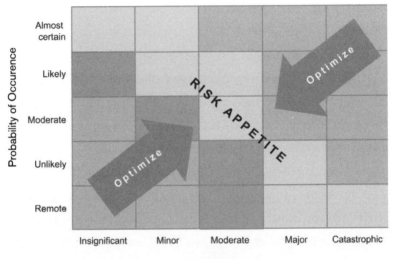

IN LIEU OF SURE THINGS

There are no sure things. But there are enough degrees of predictability, in so many instances, that we tend to be able survive and move forward. For more than half a millennium, since the late 1400s, we humans have poked at uncertainty, looking for some semblance of hidden order. We've invented new math processes and tried calculating. We've drawn pictures and tried visualizing. We observed and observed, relentlessly looking for patterns.

Risk management, in its various stages of development, is a reflection of our progressive efforts at reducing the risks of bad results and improving the odds of good ones. We invent processes that lend themselves to rational decision making, only to discover that in many instances we are not rational. We come up with new processes that factor in personal preferences to help us make less imperfect decisions. In the end, we accept that we cannot always win. Instead, we look for whatever advantages we can find to help us win a little more often.

In *Feet of Clay*, Anthony Storr writes that "doubt and uncertainty are distressing conditions from which men and women passionately desire release. . . . As a species we are intolerant of chaos and have a strong predilection for finding and inventing order."[21] However, Nobel laureate Richard Feynman says: "It is in the admission of ignorance and the admission of uncertainty that there is hope for the continuous motion of human beings in some direction that doesn't get confined, permanently blocked, as it has so many times before in various periods in the history of man." In other words, though we hate the prospect of uncertainty, our progress depends upon it.

The increasing popularity of enterprise risk management is a clear indication of the attention being paid to risks and their consequences. The return on effective risk management investment is manyfold. We can help subdue big earnings swings, keep reputations intact, maintain positive brand association, reduce litigation, avoid big market value swings, increase operational efficiency, preserve shareholder loyalty, and positively influence morale. Approached with thought and appropriate people, tools, and policies, risk management helps achieve corporate goals with fewer surprises.

As James Lam points out, the risk management decision is strictly binary: "Over the longer term, the only alternative to risk management is crisis management, and crisis management is much more embarrassing, expensive, and time-consuming."

Mitigating Pervasive Risk

CHAPTER 4

Treatment Options

"The best-laid schemes o' mice an' men gang aft a-gley. "

—Robert Burns

A ll business is risky. Logically, then, success or failure depends on a company's risk management savvy. While some may approach the management of risk with a fly swatter, the majority observe a more sophisticated approach wherein some risks are avoided, others accepted, some transferred, and others mitigated. These are the four classic risk treatments, and art and science inevitably come together in determining when and how to apply them. This chapter will present an overview of these treatment options, sprinkled with a healthy mix of executive insight, and a discussion of some of the mathematical responses that have evolved to assist with the job.

The universe is a system of complex variables whose interrelationships, where they exist, have barely been unveiled. Business is just a subset. The complex variables and unknown interrelationships persist. Nothing is certain, but many things are reasonably probable.

We all understand, viscerally, the concept of probability. The likelihood is great that our automobile trip to the local grocery store to buy a lottery ticket will be successful. The prospect of winning, on the other hand, is very unlikely. Every new strategy, marketing plan, or manufacturing retooling is littered with factors of varying probability. And every factor represents some level of gain or loss. We welcome factors of high probability of high gain. We avoid those with high probability of high loss. Most business decisions deal with the complex middle ground.

Eskimos understand snow; they have eight different words for different types of snow. Insurance companies and casinos understand risks. Policy pooling and regulations help guarantee that insurance companies will have ample funds to pay off claims from premium and investment revenues. Casinos make sure the odds are always in their favor, and either refuse or hedge "bank-breaking" bets. No businesses are more risk managed than financial services, insurance companies, and gambling establishments. Risk is their business, and to varying extents risk is everyone's business.

Therefore, in managing risk, the risks themselves must first be put in context. In other words: What categories does the risk or set of risks under discussion fall into? Are they strategic, financial, operational, regulatory, economic, and so forth? Does the risk pertain to a division or does it affect the company as a whole, and how local or widespread is its potential impact? Could it be benign on an enterprise level but serious on the divisional? These considerations place the risks in a more meaningful context.

ANTICIPATING AND FORECASTING

As head of one of the world's largest shipping, container, and transport companies, Robert Woods, CEO of P&O, spends time thinking about freight rates and how best to anticipate their fluctuation. He told us: "Risk is really about what can go wrong, and what does go wrong. And for us, what most fundamentally goes wrong is the price of the product that one is selling." The liner industry, Woods says, is one of the most economically pure. "It's classic supply and demand. There's no government regulation. It's not like airlines, where you have to have landing rights. You can put your ship in South Africa tomorrow morning. Therefore, if you're in that situation, it's about cost."

To manage his costs, Woods places great emphasis on his team's ability to look ahead. The company maintains a dedicated planning department that charts swings in world trade cycles, the capacity available during those cycles, and the implications on revenue.

"We anticipate in so far as we are able," he adds. "Bear in mind that shipping is a very long-term thing. Ships last for at least 20 years. Of course, you can charter for a lot shorter periods, but it's expensive. You have to try to look forward, and forecast, and we do. But it's a damn difficult thing to get right."

By way of example, Woods indicates, "We did anticipate oversupply last year. And, it did occur. The liner industry is a huge global industry, and there are too many firms, and not enough consolidation. So, there was precious little we could do about it and the rates came down." In response, because P&O had predicted the condition, it had already prepared a significant cost reduction "to weather the storm." Anticipating the risk, investing the time and effort into proper forecasting and planning, led to what Woods considers "the key risk analysis" in his company's business model.

In mapping a company's primary risks, management must factor in the likelihood, the level, and the loss of the risks in question. What is the probability of the risk occurring? What happens if it should occur? What is the projected impact on the company's assets—its shareholders, its finances, its property, its employees, its brand and reputation? In addition, management must be sensitive to the fact that the triggering of one risk may set in motion other risk events, so correlations must be considered. All of these must be worked through before management can determine how best to treat the given risk or risks.

Companies need to stay attuned to the interrelationship of risk. Take the possible domino effect created by an analyst industry downgrade. Bob Dellinger, the CFO of Sprint, offers this commentary: "If you look back at what happened in just the last two years, between governance issues and accounting fraud and the credit markets, and you look at what's happened to the telecom industry relative to that, you could find that all of a sudden you have a rating agency downgrade. All of a sudden, you have risk with your commercial paper. All of a sudden, you have to go into the long-term debt market. And then you find, 'Boy, that's drying up too.' There's this chain reaction of events, which had you anticipated properly, you might have managed differently. It's constantly asking yourself, 'What if?' It forces you to take some time, plan and prepare."

AVOIDANCE

There are some risks whose consequences or likelihood or organizational impact is so great, management may choose to avoid them altogether. In 1998 the knowledge management software company, ServiceWare, pulled away from its IPO plans when its bankers described the possibility of a less than successful uptake on the Street. While money from the offering would have helped ServiceWare's product development and growth plans, management knew that a failed offering would be a possible death knell. For them, postponing the IPO and avoiding the risk was a logical and prudent strategy.[1]

The ethics of cloning clearly force biotech leaders to tread cautiously, avoiding extreme and controversial technologies that could place the company under regulatory prohibition, while advancing other areas such as stem cell research that fall within more acceptable current boundaries.

On a geopolitical level, certain underdeveloped parts of the world represent very attractive untapped markets. But in areas prone to severe political or economic instability, the risks of doing business may be too great to make the opportunity worthwhile. A couple of years ago the Canadian diamond mining entity SouthernEra Resources decided to close two of its Angolan mines due to mounting security costs caused by continued UNITA rebel attacks against it and the ongoing "blood diamond" trade. A less extreme example of geopolitical rationalizing is the move by Starbucks to pull its operations out of Israel in mid-2003 due to concerns over the rising cost of security. The revenue opportunity simply was not worth the risk.[2]

The same avoidance tactic has also been extended to products. In 1976, M&M Mars responded to publicity about the carcinogenic effects of red dye number 2 by taking red M&Ms off the market. The company did this despite the fact that red M&Ms were not made with red dye number 2. Yet, because public perception ran counter to this fact, management responded out of proactive self-interest and shelved the color.[3] The scare subsequently wore off and red M&Ms were reintroduced in 1987.

As these examples illustrate, risk avoidance is generally and best resorted to in cases where the probability and consequences of the risk impact is so great as to be potentially devastating to a key corporate asset, be it a brand, finances, or people. It's worth noting that since avoidance typically involves closing down or divesting from an activity or function, management of even the most risk-averse companies should employ caution in exercising it. Applying the tourniquet needlessly can place unexpected pressure on other parts of the organization and introduce additional risks as a consequence.

ACCEPTANCE

By virtue of being in business, managers accept certain risks. As Bob Dellinger remarked: "We're a telecom company. It's not likely that we're going to become a software company in the near future. And if we decided that telecom was too risky, it would take us an extended period of time to get out."

As managers accept the risks of being in a certain line of business, they need to remain alert to intrinsic or extrinsic factors that could change the risk tolerances. After decades of profitable work in silicone breast implants, for example, the tide turned. Problems were found. Suits were filed. The risks grew and the two major manufacturers, Dow Corning and Bristol-Myers Squibb, vacated the business.

Most of the time, the risk environment undulates less sensationally but bears equal watching. A credit card company that lowers its credit threshold may enjoy the economic benefit of many more card holders while recognizing its corresponding exposure to default risk. This arrangement may constitute an acceptable and lucrative risk model. However, management would be wise to continually monitor things like public sentiment over the rate of consumer indebtedness and assess what impact a negative shift in perception of such credit lending practices might have on their business before an actual backlash can do damage to their reputations.

Ultimately, though, there are some risks you just have to take on the chin. As Bob Dellinger puts it: "There are some risks that I can hedge or protect myself from. There are some I can diversify, so I can absorb them if they happened. And there are some that you just say, 'Well, you know what, there's not much I can do about those. Those are risks I'm just going to have to live with.' However, all risk, particularly unavoidable risk, must be understood and monitored."

The same holds true for military planning, according to General Barry McCaffrey: "You've got to plan. And, then having thought through the plan with the help of your associates, you look at how it could come apart on you, and work to eliminate or mitigate the risk. Then, after you've done that, you're finally left with an element of risk where you say, 'This part of the plan is unknowable, and if it happens, here's all we can do.' That risk you must be prepared to embrace." Where a military strategist is unwilling to accept that risk, McCaffrey says, "they'll thrash around trying to find an excellent solution instead of the best solution," and run the risk of undue delay or, worse, being blindsided. "It's the definable risk I can live with," McCaffrey adds resolutely.

MITIGATE

When mitigating a risk, management looks for an approach that reduces either the likelihood or the consequences of the risk event. When a lawsuit is settled rather than battled in court, a company is usually seeking to mitigate its exposure. The pain is not eliminated since the company generally makes some accommodation to the plaintiff, but the severity is lessened.

John Wren, CEO of Omnicom, mitigated his company's vulnerability to the dot-com rise and fall by permitting his advertising agencies to perform work for those businesses only insofar as Omnicom's advertising agencies leased no additional office space or other long-term capital commitments to execute it. This ran counter to the practices of many other agencies at the peak of the bubble. But where these same businesses were hit hard by the subsequent implosion of dot-com advertising, Omnicom suffered less.

Brent Callinicos, Microsoft's treasurer and a seasoned and highly respected risk manager, comments that "it's too easy to look at risk in a two-dimensional way." When it comes to reducing the probability and impact of risk, you need to look hard at the real world. The best way to do that, says Callinicos, "given you don't have the capital market's ability to correlate risks from having thousands and thousands of data points over a given period of time," is to look at other companies and find out what has happened to them. "Take the loss of key executives," he adds. "Go out and find a company that's experienced a sudden departure." Then study that company's response. Research public reaction. Examine how the market moved. Then use that experience and those data points to develop your own response.

If a significant portion of your business is conducted through foreign operations, Jeff Clarke, Hewlett-Packard's head of operations, says to be watchful for evolving market economies such as those in Eastern Europe. In shielding the larger enterprise from the risks of conducting business in those areas, Clarke says you need to "be extremely vigilant around the Foreign Corrupt Practices Act and on relationships between countries that ship into markets such as prewar

Iraq or Cuba, where regional sensitivities may be different from the sensitivities of companies headquartered in the United States."

Whatever management deems as its primary risk set, risk mitigation is fundamentally about protecting a company's agility. As an entity's strategic responsibilities bubble and shift, management is wise to preemptively dull those edges that could puncture its ability to execute as planned.

TRANSFER

By transferring a risk, a company solicits the involvement of a third party to take on some of the impact should a risk event occur. While mergers and acquisitions, joint ventures, and other partnerships are often formed to satisfy a risk transfer need, the role is most commonly played by the insurer. Indeed, risk transference in the form of insurance has existed for thousands of years.

Moses was reputed to have asked the Israelites to contribute a portion of their produce for alien residents, widows, and orphans. And even before that, Babylon's Code of Hammurabi included a form of credit insurance.[4]

The famous Lloyd's of London wasn't an insurance house, it was a coffeehouse belonging to Edward Lloyd, where merchants and bankers met informally to do business. Specific amounts of seafaring risk were posted on a wallboard, and financiers willing to accept any posted risk in return for a "premium" would write their names underneath it. As a result we have the term "underwriters."

Bob Dellinger was formerly CEO of GE Frankona Re. As a reinsurer, Dellinger says: "You learn to accept only those risks that can be understood and modeled." This is because there needs to be some way to quantify what's at stake and the range of possible returns. Then, adds Dellinger, "you put probabilities against those returns. You calculate things like the odds of a tidal wave hitting Ireland. You do a one-in-100-year model, and you say the odds are 0.001 of a tidal wave hitting Ireland. And then you put a price around that and say, 'How much of that risk am I willing to take on the off chance that this is the year in which it happens? Does the return justify the risk and can I absorb the worst case loss?'"

After the 1989, Loma Prieta earthquake in the San Francisco Bay area, and the Northridge earthquake near Los Angeles in 1994, several insurers were no longer offering earthquake policies because of cumulative losses suffered from both events. Earthquake policies are relatively expensive and have typical deductibles of 10 percent of the value of the dwelling. For San Francisco Bay area residential real estate, with average prices of $466,000 in August 2003, many people shudder at the prospect of shelling out $47,000 and more on top of costly annual premiums in the event of a total loss. As a result, the number of policies is relatively small, creating even higher premiums and deductibles. In this situation the numbers don't work very well.

Insurance is not a blanket protection. Brent Callinicos illustrates this point: "Often the business person doesn't recognize they're taking a risk. Some risks can be passed on to somebody else and some risks can rightfully be assumed."

The point, he stresses, is that "the business model must be economically appealing. Our job [in treasury] is to figure out the best way to mitigate the risk, and buying insurance isn't the default. The default is to pass the risk on to somebody else. If you can't do that, then you take the risk on yourself and determine a way to live with the risk that helps the business strategically." A business unit head may have flexibilities—whether from exerting contractual muscle or from a product standpoint—that it could have overlooked by turning to insurance reflexively.

As with all risk responses, the cost of a risk transfer must also be considered. Clearly, when the cost of insurance exceeds tolerable limits, the company must either swallow the risk or find some other answer.

Callinicos would agree: "We're not chomping at the bit to go buy insurance for everything that we can. And often there are things you can't buy insurance for. Reputational risk is one of those. That's where the invitation comes to pass. We often discover things whereby the solution is something we will work on with a bunch of other groups . . . and we'll say there's a risk that we can't deal with here in our insurance capacity. Let's make sure we find and talk to and educate the people who can. We recognize that we're not always able to help put the solution in place, but we can help to raise the right questions."

Whatever risk treatment one eventually adopts, it is worth noting that there will likely be some level of residual risk, some leftover stain that must be accepted, shrugged off, or treated at some future date. This should be documented and communicated to all relevant parties. By the same token, all assumptions made about the risk or its treatment should likewise be put in print and shared.

SHAPING RISK: MATHEMATICAL TOOLS AND RESPONSES

The Rise of Derivatives

Is there any way to separate the probabilities of something and the payoff related to it? Can we skew the payoff so a downside is capped but an upside is unbounded? We can, and we do—through derivatives.

There is nothing new about derivatives. Aristotle, in his book *Politics*, written 2500 years ago, mentions an option on the use of olive-oil presses. In the 1700s the Japanese traded futures-like contracts on rice or warehouse receipts. And the Chicago Board of Trade has been the scene of forward and futures contract trading since 1849. Derivatives get their name because their prices are "derived" from the price of some underlying security or commodity, or an index, interest rate, or exchange rate. The term "derivative" includes forwards, futures, options, swaps, combinations of such, and combinations plus traditional securities and loans. Here are some definitions:

Forward contracts, the original and most basic derivative form, are agreements to buy or sell a certain quantity of an asset or commodity in the future, at a specified price, time, and place.

Futures are standardized agreements to buy or sell a certain quantity of an asset or commodity in the future at a specified price, time, and place. They differ from forward contracts in that they're standardized as to quantity, the underlying assets or commodities, and the time. Only the price and number of contracts are negotiated in the trading process. A daily margining system limits the risk of default.

Options have already been described, and these give the buyers the right, but not the obligation, to buy or sell an asset or commodity at a specified "strike" price on or before a certain date. "Call" options are options to buy; "put" options are options to sell. Options sellers have the obligation to pay when buyers exercise their rights.

Swaps are agreements to swap the net value of two series of payments in which one is usually based on a fixed interest rate and the other is linked to a variable interest rate, another currency's interest rate, the total rate of return of a security or index, or a commodity price.

Notional values are the amounts used to calculate the payoff. These values can be staggering, but the actual liabilities are much lower. For example, the Bank of International Settlements, in 1995, found that the notional values of all derivatives (excluding those traded in organized exchanges) was $41 trillion; however, if every obligated party reneged, creditor loss would have been only $1.7 trillion, or 4.3 percent of the notional value.

We are all familiar with the normal probability distribution curve, or bell-shaped curve, where the occurrence of values falls symmetrically on both sides of the average. In the ideal case, the likelihood of values some magnitude below average is equal to that of values above average. So, if we were considering a share of stock with what we believed was an average price of $50, the likelihood of the price falling to $45 would be the same as its rising to $55. Buying shares at $50 would be a coin toss.

But suppose you felt certain that the share prices would rise over some time period, and suppose for $250 you could buy the right, but not the obligation, to buy 100 shares at $50 each. If before the end of that period the shares were selling for $60, you could buy and then sell the 100 shares and pocket $750 ($1000 – $250). On the other hand, suppose, during that period, the shares never reached $50. In this case you end up losing $250. Here, we have symmetric underlying distribution with an asymmetric payoff. The odds of a $10 move up or down were 50/50, but the payoff was +$750/–$250.

Clearly, there's lots of money to be lost by buyers and sellers if the options are not priced appropriately. Seat-of-the-pants pricing over the centuries—since at least the 1600s, in fact—made options themselves a speculative proposition. It was not until the late 1960s that a repeatable, consistent solution was devised. Fischer Black, Myron Scholes, and Robert Merton provided a solution that depended upon four elements: time, price spread (or more particularly, the ratio between the stock price and the strike price), interest rates, and volatility.

So, although the derivative itself is not new, the availability of an accurate pricing formula was the new breakthrough. While books can (and have) been written—and in the case of Messrs. Black and Scholes, Nobel prizes won—unlocking the mathematical underpinnings of the formula, the achievement provided a previously impossible level of precision to options pricing. Indeed, since its introduction in the mid-'70s, Black-Scholes has fueled much of the subsequent rise in the popularity and use of derivatives.

This example of options pricing illustrates the concept: An option to buy one share of AT&T stock over the period June 6, 1995, through October 15, 1995, cost $2.50. The current price was $50, and the strike price was $50.25. No matter how far below $50.25 the share price could fall, the buyer's loss is capped at $2.50. If the share price increases above $50.25 to $52.74, the buyer would still gain less than $2.50. Once the stock price goes above $52.75, the upside is theoretically infinite. The $2.50 option price was primarily dictated by the market's expectation that AT&T share prices would be more likely than not to stay within a five-point range, or 10 percent, during that four-month period.

At that same time, Microsoft shares were selling for $83¹/₈, and you could buy an option over that same period, with a strike price of $90, for $4.50. Here, the strike price was nearly seven points away from the current price, compared with only a spread of $0.25 for the AT&T option. The market expectation at the time was for Microsoft share prices to be more volatile than AT&T's, and the option pricing reflected this.

The size of the derivatives market is proof of its efficacy. The Bank of International Settlements estimated that derivative settlements in 1998 exceeded $109 trillion in outstanding contracts and over $400 trillion in trading volumes on derivatives exchanges.[5] The complexity of the market has also increased exponentially.

Many of today's derivative products are combinations of the derivative fundamentals mentioned at the beginning of this section. Their pricing is also far more complex than can be calculated using the Black-Scholes formula. Public market derivatives cover a broad enough scope to entice the buyers and speculators necessary to their proper function.

Some of the new derivatives, though, are customized to particular customers and their very specific needs. A petroleum company with risk of loss due to falling oil prices might be matched with airline companies whose risk of loss is tied to rising oil prices. If the price of oil falls, the petroleum company's downside is reduced by the derivative, while the airline's cost of its derivative premiums are covered in part by the increased operating profits that accrue from the lower fuel prices. Where oil prices are rising, the petroleum company's derivative premium costs are compensated by its increased profitability, and the airline companies' operating losses are buffered by the increased value of the derivative.

Hedging for Risk Limitation: Lessons from P&O

"You could say we should have predicted it," Robert Woods of P&O says. "We all thought the price of oil would go down after the end of the Iraq war, and it has not. It has gone up.

And that is a big risk to us, and impacts seriously on our bottom line."

"And then there are the currencies too," Woods adds, "because the euro has strengthened against the U.S. dollar by 15 percent in the last 12 months . . . ."[6]

For Woods and P&O, the risk limitations offered through hedging are an advantage. The company spends a lot of money hedging oil prices. Fortunately for P&O, Woods notes, "we could see that there were all sorts of issues with the dollar, and that it would decline, and so we hedged against the dollar. We use hedging as a safety net, rather than a profit center. We did that at the end of the last year when we did our budget. We were comfortable with the level of the oil price at the end of October, and so we took out a hedge against that oil price because the risk of it going wrong would torpedo our budget. And because of it, we actually did well out of that market hedge."

Sometimes it may not be possible to fully balance the risk with complementary buyers. In that case, the financial institutions brokering the derivatives act as speculators covering those portions of the imbalances. By appropriate pricing, it's a win-win-win, so long as the companies buying the derivatives are using them to hedge. If they use them to speculate, the consequences can be extreme.

But derivatives are a tool. Used appropriately, they can provide sound hedging versatility. Frank Knight, professor of economics at the University of Iowa and the University of Chicago, remarks: "Every act of production is a speculation in the relative value of money, and the good produced."

Derivatives do not reduce the risks associated with owning volatile assets. What they do is determine who will take on the speculation and who will avoid it.

VALUE AT RISK

Andy Grove, erstwhile chairman of the Intel Corporation, was known for having stated that what can be measured can be improved. In *Agile Business for Fragile Times*, we pointed out that one of the problems associated with aligning business processes with strategy was a tendency to measure the wrong things because you could, and then build monitoring systems around those measurements.

The financial industry created its own tools, known as "value at risk," or VaR, to depict risk and exposure. While no silver bullet, VaR is recognized for being a necessary and helpful instrument in making better financial decisions.

Value at risk is defined as the potential loss of monetary value over a period of time at a given probability. But there are lots of debates about defining it in practice. Some of these, Dan Borge says, are: "Should we pick a one-year time period or a one-day time period? Should we pick a 1 percent probability level or a 5 percent level? What is the starting point to measure the loss, today's value, the value expected at the end of the chosen time period, or some other value? The list goes on. . . ."[7]

VaR is not precise but it is quantitative, and many say it's better than having no measure at all. Here's an example of how it works: We want to assess the worst-case overnight position with 95 percent degree of confidence. A portfolio managing $100 million might have a 95 percent probability of losing up to $4 million in value overnight. Its VaR, as a percent of assets, is 4 percent. To compare the riskiness of different portfolios, and the risk-adjusted results of their managers, let's examine two funds starting the year at $100 million. The first manager's average overnight 95 percent VaR was $7 million, or 7 percent of assets. The second manager's average overnight 95 percent VaR was $2 million, or 2 percent of assets. Manager one earns a return of 30 percent. Manager two earns 20 percent. In risk-adjusted terms, manager two's results were better, because manager one put comparably more at risk.

A critical adjunct to VaR is stress testing. By picking scenarios that attack relevant portfolio weak points, such as a disproportionate percent of foreign currency exposure, risk managers can stress test the portfolio and have a better picture of value at risk under difficult market conditions. With this added information, managers can see under what conditions the portfolio's risk profile falls outside the intended risk-appetite level.

VaR has become a widely accepted risk measure in the financial community and is being touted more broadly as a way of measuring the risks of nonfinancial companies. But the concepts, variables, and formulas that work reasonably well in the financial industry are yet to be proven as effective in nonfinancial industries.

One danger is to look at risk management as a way to systematize the process and take gut-level factors out of the equation. On the contrary, risk evaluation has to take risk appetite into account, so gut-level factors can never be expunged from the process. The VaR formula, however, does not take risk appetite into account, so it has to be used in conjunction with other measures that do.

CONCLUSION: DECISIONS, DECISIONS . . .

An important manifestation of effective risk management is getting a handle on the scope, volatilities, and severities of the risks one's company faces, then tailoring an appropriate set of risk responses. Risk managers have many types of risk treatments at their disposal. Every company's risk management "solution" will be unique because the exposures and risk appetites all differ. The key is to have a reasonable understanding of how each treatment option works, alone and in combination with others, so that decisions are informed and results are less influenced by luck than by reason.

CHAPTER 5

The Numbers Game— Responding to Financial Risk

"Take calculated risks. That is quite different from being rash."

—George Patton

Financial risk can include the failure of financial systems from instances of credit risk and market risk. It can also include regulatory failures and compliance issues. Through sound financial risk management, companies can evaluate business strategies that are appropriate to their strategic, operational, and financial risk tolerance. They can model the variability and interaction of business risks, the relationships between products and services, and the effect of risk control mechanisms such as pricing, insurance, and dividend policy. They can then establish key performance indicators derived from the financial models that management can use to monitor the outcomes of the scenarios being modeled or analyzed. This chapter looks at credit risk and market risk and the implications and responses of each.

CREDIT RISK

In a slow economy, credit risk becomes a particular concern as companies write off increasing amounts of bad debt. Cisco set aside $288 million for bad accounts in the year ending July 2001, a figure nearly seven times higher than it had set aside only one year before, according to an article by *CFO Magazine*.[1] Not surprisingly, executives are training their attention on receivables management.

While accelerating credit collection is sound policy, clamping down on the credit window is not straightforward. Simply printing strict new terms on an invoice ignores the subtleties between credit policy and the customer relationship. Key customers appreciate greater leniency in the billing and processing of late payments. Accommodating this can go far to foster goodwill and build the relationship. Credit policy is also a competitive instrument. The company that can offer less restrictive credit terms is likely to attract more customers and increased share. Yet, it's a fine line, and finance executives must accord the right firmness when dealing with the majority of its contracts so its customers pay within the targeted range.

The financial and credit history of one's customers are two important elements of a company's credit term assessment. The overall economic climate is another. Nancy Cheng used to be the finance director at the Asian headquarters of Columbia TriStar, distributor of such television hits as *Seinfeld* and *Jeopardy*. In response to the 1997 Asian financial crisis, Cheng sat down with her team of credit managers to rework payment terms with its broadcasters, many of whom were struggling from the weakened advertising market and had not met the 60 day days-sales-outstanding limit. Cheng and her team took the business view that since other vendors were also likely clamoring for payment, it was better for all concerned to cut the broadcasters some slack rather than run the companies into extinction. Thus, they made the decision to extend payment terms and in some cases to reduce the original purchase price.[2] Columbia TriStar gained some goodwill and increased its odds of getting some payment, and its broadcasters gained some breathing room.

Microsoft also stepped up its relationships from that of merely vendor to business partner, through its Microsoft Capital customer financing program launched in the fall of 2002. Microsoft developed the financing program specifically for small and medium-size businesses in order to make it easier for them to purchase end-to-end solutions. Microsoft Capital provides complete financing, offering both term loans and operating leases. The move was made for strategic rather than tactical reasons. Brent Callinicos, Microsoft's treasurer, explains: "We didn't want to provide financing just because we had cash. We wanted it to advantage our business. We were very deliberate about that." Unlike traditional financial services firms, Microsoft has no leverage risk from its lending. As for credit risk, Callinicos states: "We are very careful about the credit we take and we do our homework and make sure that the right checks are done. But all told, it has been a very successful and strategic move for the company."

Other companies are resorting to charging interest on overdue balances in order to bring discipline into the credit and liquidity balance. This arrangement suits customers who would prefer longer payment windows and don't mind paying a little on top for the benefit. It is also effective in discouraging what might otherwise be a spiraling pattern of delinquencies. The converse works as well. Companies that offer a discount to early paying customers sometimes find it an attractive inducement, netting positive results.

While nurturing key customer relationships is important, seasoned finance executives also realize that where customers have gone awry in past bill paying, a firm hand must be applied so future credit terms are respected. They refrain from shipping subsequent orders until prior bills are paid, and require their customers to put down a deposit or provide a letter of credit. As Nancy Cheng said of TriStar in her interview with CFO Magazine: "We give them reasonable terms so they can keep their shops open, but we also want to make sure there are incentives for us to keep the relationship going."

Effective receivables management ultimately depends on clearly articulating and enforcing the company's credit policies both to customers as well as one's sales staff. The latter is important in order to avoid undue discounting or rule bending to meet sales and commissions quotas. Such policies need the involvement and approval from the organization's CFO. Given how inextricably tied credit management is to sound cashflow and the operation of a sound business, such management is enmeshed in the CFO's stewardship responsibilities.

In terms of continuous improvement, Oracle CFO Jeff Henley says: "We benchmark our accounts payable department and talk to people and we try to figure out, 'Are we being efficient?'" Of course, he adds, "you always try to benchmark quality." If you're in the financial function, he notes, "you can be cheap." However: "You can be running a low-cost finance group, but are you providing good internal controls? Are you providing good analytic services?

"It's an age old problem," Henley admits, "but the best way I know how to do it is through networking, benchmarking, talking to other people, and," he adds, "if you're old like me, You draw on your experience."

One metric Henley relies on is finance costs as a percentage of revenue: "You know if your finance cost as a percentage of revenue is dropping, and you are making improvements." He adds that every company faces "the tradeoff of efficiency coming at the expense of weakening internal controls or not providing good levels of service." In response, he notes, "you draw upon your experience. You draw upon benchmarking. You draw on your auditors' comment. You get an awful lot of comment from people to help you determine if you're doing a good job."

In refining one's credit policies and guidelines, here are some things to keep in mind:

☐ Do your homework on your customers. Far more money will be saved in the long run. Use credit bureaus to analyze financial and credit history. Supplement these reports with news tracking, examination of SEC filings, and in person discussions where possible.

☐ Examine current credit policies to see if they need to be refreshed. Confirm that guidelines are clearly communicated and understood among finance, marketing, and sales staff.

☐ Discourage end of quarter discounting. It may take tough love at first, but communicate to staff that linear quarterly sales are the expectation and that additional discounting or incentives need top management approval.

☐ Conduct a receivables management exercise. Determine what percentage of your customers is regularly in arrears. Meet with them personally to explore the underlying reasons. Adjust their payment program to ensure that future payments are realized—possibly extend terms, lower the purchase price, offer channel incentives, and use one's own network to sell overstock. Then lock down on future ordering and billing practices to prevent a recurring pattern of delinquent payments—require deposit or pay-down, a credit letter, or other guarantee.

☐ Understand that credit management is a competitive tool. Be aware of current practices within your industry. Remember that having a personal relationship with key customers makes their retention more assured.

☐ Make sure the CFO takes overall responsibility for enforcing credit guidelines, particularly in overseas jurisdictions where problems can easily arise.

☐ Consider using or paying attention to what the credit derivatives market has to say about your clients and key vendors.

MARKET RISK

Market risks, which included interest rates, foreign exchange rates, commodity prices, and equity prices, inject uncertainty into one's business and impact a company's ability to project future costs and returns. To counteract these forces, the financial markets rely on derivative instruments.

As previously discussed, financial derivatives, most commonly comprising forwards, futures, swaps, and options, have grown at a remarkable rate over the past decade. Interest rate swaps and financial futures started growing rapidly in the '80s. Today, company officers have at their disposal the means to hedge risks in ways that were not available in the past. Advances in options theory and the mathematics behind complex financial products combined with a surge in the quality and accessibility of sophisticated computing and communications technology have succeeded in opening up an array of hedging strategies. Once the purview of the chosen in what was primarily the financial field, these opportunities are now broadly disseminated.

Derivatives can work like insurance as a means to transfer financial risks. Like auto or home insurance, derivatives serve as a valuable risk management tool to cost effectively and efficiently protect your assets against future events. For corporate treasury departments, they are actively deployed to manage: interest rate risk, foreign currency (FX) risk, and equity risk. A description of each class follows.

Interest Rate Risk

Most companies are affected by interest risk whether through debt management/funding requirements, corporate pension plans, or other investments. The finance chief's goal is to shelter these assets, or liabilities, from unfavorable rate exposure. Some companies, for example, have floating rate loans tied to LIBOR (London InterBank Offered Rate). If your company had a seven-year floating rate loan priced at one month LIBOR, you would be exposed to upward movements in the monthly LIBOR rate. To hedge the upside interest-rate risk, you might enter into an "interest rate swap." This is an agreement to exchange at specific future dates a series of variable rate payments for a series of fixed rate payments, or vice versa. By entering into the swap, your company would make the fixed interest payments over the life of the swap and receive floating rate payments in return. Thus, if LIBOR rises as the company expects, it is shielded.

In our present market, with its low interest rates, any hedging needs to be done before the rates rise. To do so, a company might take out a short (or sell) position on a short-term interest-rate futures contract. If interest rates rise, the price of their futures contract will fall, and a gain would be made on the exchange, since the holder of the contract would be required to pay the company. The gain the company would have made on their futures position would offset the increased cost of their planned borrowing. By the same token, should interest rates fall, the company would net a loss on its futures contract. However, this loss in turn would be offset by the company's gain of borrowing at a lower interest rate.

Other examples abound. Companies managing large pension plans or investment portfolios manage their market risk through interest rate and equity based derivatives and have a range of hedging formulas available to assist them.

Things to consider in managing interest-rate risk are:

☐ Keep frequent watch on leading indicators that may presage unexpected rate swings.

☐ Adjust debt-to-equity ratios to reflect anticipated rate trends.

☐ Hedge to help reduce volatility.

Foreign Currency Risk

Any company conducting business overseas understands that trading and operating in foreign jurisdictions means incurring costs and revenues in nonparallel currencies. A goal for finance executives is to minimize the shock of foreign currency movements on corporate business strategy.

A Taiwanese exporter typically manufactures their product at home, but exports the bulk overseas and is paid in U.S. dollars. Its costs are local, however, and must be paid in Taiwanese dollars. But the exchange rate between the U.S. dollar and the Taiwan dollar fluctuates, and sometimes significantly. To deal with the uncertainty, the Taiwanese manufacturer might consider taking out a forward contract.

A forward contract involves company management agreeing on the price at which an asset will be bought or sold at some future date. In our example, the Taiwanese manufacturer might agree on a forward contract to sell their U.S. dollars at a rate of 34 Taiwanese dollars for one U.S. dollar in one year's time. In this case, the underlying asset is the U.S. dollar. By signing the forward contract, the Taiwanese company locks in the value of its future export sales and removes the uncertainty about future profits.

FMC, a large manufacturer of agricultural, specialty, and industrial chemicals, provides another example. In the late '80s, FMC had grown to include facilities in 15 different countries. A full third of its $3.3 billion sales revenue came from these international locations. One of these—its Irish subsidiary—manufactured an ingredient included in aspirin tablets that it sold to European aspirin manufacturers. The environment in which this business competed made its market share vulnerable to upward movements in the U.S. dollar compared against the Irish punt. To protect its market share, FMC employed forward contracts and currency options to hedge against the risk of a rising dollar. The accrued gains went back to the Irish subsidiary, which permitted it not to raise prices and to stake a further competitive foothold despite a stronger dollar.[3]

During the mid 1990s the Mexican currency devaluation placed many of Microsoft's Mexican distributors on soft footing. In an article for *International Reports*, Brent

Callinicos, Microsoft's treasurer, was quoted saying: "Since we are the ones with the deepest pocket in the food chain, we're often forced to step in and help distributors." When we asked Callinicos about the program, he told us: "It's a way in which we can deploy our treasury expertise on the capital markets side to strategically help our business."

In fact, since Microsoft bills in non-U.S. currencies in many locations, including Mexico, the argument could be made that Microsoft was itself exposed to the sting of the devaluation. As Callinicos adds: "We're a dollar based company. We bring the money back eventually." Still, he feels this view is myopic. Instead, he says, you could flip the arrangement and bill in dollars, even though the distributor will turn around and sell in local currency.

Even so, Callinicos warns that an unsuspecting company can get caught in unpleasant snares. "It works fine," he says, "as long as nothing happens to the currency during that time period. However, if the currency devalues, like it did in Brazil or Southeast Asia, a few things happen. One, they are living on 2 to 5 percent margins, so they go bankrupt. This is not good for us because we don't have a direct touch with the customers. Or, two, they can turn around and look at us and say, 'Okay, you're making 90 percent margins, what are you going to do for me?' Or the third thing that can happen is that they pay up but they stop buying anything. And they'll just sit on what they have so they can raise prices later. And we've seen this in Southeast Asia."

Callinicos cautions those companies who take only the two-dimensional view. These companies may feel they are protected by selling in dollars, and don't see the latent risk. But he stresses that the companies do have that risk. "We as Microsoft had an implicit risk as a result of the part we play in the hierarchy of that sale." In their case, Callinicos states, "we turn it around and say, 'Is there something we can do to help our local subsidiaries?' As a result, we're now on version two or version three of what we refer to as our local currency price protection program."

From that program, Microsoft was able to turn what could have been a bothersome foreign exchange risk into a competitive advantage. It took the path of risk optimization to alleviate the exposure of its distributors, resellers, and subsidiaries to the risk of those devaluations. Callinicos remarks: "We saw periods of time after we put this program in place where there were devaluations, where our competitors' sales went right down to nothing and ours actually increased. We were not losing money because we had the expertise in treasury to be able to deal with it. We were hedging on their behalf and were able to pass the benefit on to them. We got a lot of customer goodwill out of it."

Moving beyond those examples, some emerging best practices for large multinational corporations make managing liquidity today much easier than in the past. Among these is the evolution of treasury centers into internal banking units. Such internal banks allow local or regional subsidiaries to electronically place foreign exchange and money market transactions through an internal electronic trading platform. The advantages inherent are that it:

- ☐ Allows the company greater and more unified control of its funds

- ☐ Allows the company to automatically integrate financial, accounting, and treasury information through one platform—some even automatically process hedging information into FAS 133 general ledger tools

- ☐ Allows the company to itself offer subsidiaries the ability to internally execute spot, forward, and future contracts

- ☐ Allows the company to manage unit loans and deposits, and gives the company greater control to shift excess funds from surplus regions to other units with cash demands

- ☐ Provides company management with a comprehensive, real-time view of its FX exposures

- ☐ Allows considerable cost-saving through sharply reduced external banking transaction fees

Another practice multinationals are taking advantage of is regional or pan-regional pooling. Although cross-border pooling still remains heavily regulated, such pooling allows companies to move their funds in U.S. dollars on a near constant and real-time basis.

Centralized risk management relations with external banks underlie most sophisticated treasury programs. To mitigate exposure, executives use single-bank and multibank trading platforms to hedge their foreign exchange positions. These platforms offer straight-through processing to aid and control risk management. In addition, leading treasury departments cushion themselves further by automatically investing balances in overnight investment instruments or placing surplus funds in investment grade U.S. commercial paper, which add additional protections against negative currency volatility.

Leaders such as Nokia also insist on monthly reporting from each of their subsidiaries on their respective foreign exposure. Their reporting cycle plots expected FX positions and related exposure over a 12-month period, calculates the net, and then hedges that total net position.[4] Tools such as value-at-risk (VaR), discussed in the previous chapter, and stress testing supplement Nokia's risk management efforts.

In managing foreign exchange risks, think about your:

☐ Direct exposure through sales in foreign currencies

☐ Indirect exposure through intermediaries' changing risks

☐ Hedging to reduce volatility

Equity Risk

Finance leaders turn to derivatives to protect the value of existing stock holdings or other exposures, such as employee stock options or loan securities, as well as to limit exposure to changes in equity prices and protect equity positions.

Concentrated equity positions are one source of risk. By concentrated, we are referring to single stock positions that represent 20 percent or more of net worth. Such positions typically occur in the event of stock-for-stock acquisitions, through a family transfer, when an otherwise diversified portfolio witnesses an unusually significant uptick in value, or in cases of stock-based compensation.

In general, sound equity risk management provides companies with concentrated stock positions the ability to:

☐ Protect against stock downturns, and thereby protect capital

☐ Diversify holdings from a single stock to a different asset

☐ Monetize the value of a stock position to generate additional liquidity

☐ Possibly defer the capital gains tax from a stock sale

Equity collars are probably the most widely used hedging strategy. For example, a company can enter into a zero-premium equity collar, struck by purchasing a put on the stock that defines the downside limit the company is willing to tolerate (say a maximum drop of 10 percent of the current share price). At the same time, the company also sells a call on the same stock at a higher-than-market price. This is adjusted so the gain from the one will exactly offset the loss from the other—thus effectively collaring the impact of future share price movements. Once collared, the shares are more secure, so they can often serve as collateral that the company can borrow against. Even with this, leading risk management practice suggests placing concentration risk limits by company, geography, industry, and risk grade.

Diversified equity holdings, unless specifically designed for speculative purposes, should be risk weighted according to the company's own tolerance levels. Likewise, the overall asset blend of bonds and equity holdings should be balanced according to market projections, investment goals, and corporate risk appetite. Operating divisions of a company may also want to hedge commodity risk, either for ingredients, general overhead (such as energy), or their product.

In managing equity risk, consider:

☐ Restructuring the equity portfolio using portfolio-management correlations to augment diversification

☐ Watching for concentrations that exceed your tolerances

THE MACRO PERSPECTIVE

While still not for the uninitiated, legal parameters have evolved to protect participants from some of the credit risk related to the use of derivatives through the increased use of collateral agreements and netting procedures. In fact, as Alan Greenspan noted: "These increasingly complex financial instruments have especially contributed, particularly over the past couple of stressful years, to the development of a far more flexible, efficient and resilient financial system than existed just a quarter century ago."[5]

The Federal Reserve also believes that the use of derivative instruments in managing market risk has helped distribute the economic shock of the major corporate defaults and, on a geopolitical level, softened the blows of the Argentinean and other economic crises. Risks have been spread and hedged among more parties, so that while many institutions may have felt pain, many fewer were affected critically.

This is not to say that such risks have been eradicated; rather, it indicates they were shared among a more diverse set of financial parties with different leverage horizons. Whereas in the past, banks with relatively short-term leverage holdings managed the bulk of the derivative trade, default swaps and other tools are now frequently passed from banks to longer-term leverage holders such as pension funds and insurers.

The credit derivatives market has risen in significance both because of its ability to spread risk and because it offers better risk management capabilities to managers as a result of their structure. For some derivatives, such as credit default swaps, the pricing already calibrates the probability of a net loss from one of the parties' defaulting. Yet, as Greenspan also noted: "Leveraging always carries with it the remote possibility of a chain reaction, a cascading sequence of defaults that will culminate in financial implosion if it proceeds unchecked. Only a central bank, with its unlimited power to create money, can with a high probability thwart such a process before it becomes destructive."[6]

Several organizations interested in financial reporting have become increasingly concerned by the relatively weak reporting on market risk in company financials. The American Institute of Certified Public Accountants noted that shareholders and other interested parties might not have understood the ultimate risk. Among other things, these constituents were unable to determine what financial instruments the company had entered into, how many of those instruments were standard, which were newer inventions, and what were the terms. Further, they complained that such confusion meant they were unable to ascertain what new risks the company had transferred or taken on and how those various arrangements were being accounted for.

REPORTING AND FINANCIAL STATEMENT RISK

There has been much discussion in the press about the need for greater financial disclosure. While well-intentioned, some of this zeal has resulted in companies presenting reams of information that do little to alleviate investor concern: clear and ready access to the primary risks impacting shareholder value.

While the ebb and flow between overdisclosure and underdisclosure is to be expected as words like "transparency" and what it means are sorted through, it is a subject that engenders energetic discussion.

"I do not think shareholders or analysts should be surprised," says HP board member and Progress & Freedom Foundation Chairman, Jay Keyworth, "and therefore, I think that disclosure should be limited as much as possible to those things that describe real, measurable, describable risks." Indeed, says Microsoft's Scott Di Valerio, financial statements are about "capturing transactions as they are intended from a revenue standpoint." The key questions in his mind are things like: "Are we reporting our transactions the way we should? Are we reporting them in a way that helps shareholders understand more about the company, more about the decisions and judgments that we make as we go through and evaluate those risks and convert those into our decisions?"

This line of thinking is inarguable. But logic dictates that quality reporting is only as good as the quality of the underlying information. The nuance it raises, however, is the distinction between meaningful information and rote disclosure. "Everybody and his brother discloses potential litigation," Keyworth says. "This is an old hat thing. We all do this. And it's not very sensitive either. Maybe HP's been a lucky case, but I really don't think our stock has fluctuated one way or the other because of any disclosures we've had about potential litigation." But he says: "We have done it assiduously because it's been part of the process."

The main point, however, is: "You've got to disclose the major areas of business risk."

For some companies, it might mean disclosing the possible risks associated with their international tax situation. For others, it could mean providing information about a significant risk concentration in a product or geography. And for still others, it could mean disclosing a particular reliance on a company's research, research on which your company is dependent for the success of a planned product or initiative.

To assist management in mitigating financial statement and reporting risk, auditors interact with audit committees and management to help identify the critical elements in their business environment. The risk and controls environment may be compared against stated goals, benchmark data, and other appropriate measures defined by company management, to see where recommendations for improvements may be made.

Ultimately, transparency requires an informed and educated management team. Given the new emphasis on nonfinancial metrics, Jeff Clarke of HP notes that Wall Street analysts are paying closer heed to indicators like channel checks—an independent stock analysis whereby company information is supplied by third parties, as opposed to the company itself—and quality-of-earnings reviews on things such as accounting reserves and segment reporting. But, says Clarke, the most important change he has observed is, "frankly, an increased understanding of these factors by management, and a consequently greater willingness for them to go into detail on nonfinancial metrics with investors as a consequence of this raised consciousness."

Microsoft's Di Valerio has had a similar experience. Prior to the company reorganizing into seven business groups, and before Sarbanes-Oxley, he said, most of the company's business groups had little interest or dealings in U.S. GAAP or external reporting. Today, he says, "they have to have a good sense for both. They now see their role as making sure that they understand how what is going on in their business impacts the external financial statements, and that proper controls including security and authorizations are being driven down all the way through the worldwide organization."

Guidance

Since transparency concerns external communication to the investment community, similar considerations must go into the question of whether to provide guidance to analysts. Some companies, like Coca-Cola and AT&T, have simply decided not to provide earnings guidance, in a move aimed at encouraging analysts to focus on the longer-term horizons. Indeed, the decision of whether to stay in or pull out of the guidance arena has emerged as a hot topic of debate.

For her part, says Pattie Dunn, HP director and vice chairman of Barclays Global Investors: "I think it's very tempting to get out of the earnings guidance game and it's something that I think every board does talk about." She adds: "It's easy to get cynical." On the positive side: "It's good to have a relationship. It's quid pro quo in a very constructive way. We're helping you do your job and you're going to help sell our story to investors and those are all plusses." But "on the negative side, it ends up being just a big game and you're trying to signal what the Street can expect without giving more than it should expect to know." In the end, Dunn concludes, "I think I have to come down on the side that says I don't feel very strongly about it."

Ken West, on the other hand, does feel strongly. "I sometimes think that First Call is among a company's worst enemies," he told us candidly. This is because "First Call accumulates earnings forecasts for the next quarter, and if the company misses by a few pennies, the market can react violently." His concern is that this leads to harmful short-term mind-sets among management and equally harmful short-term mind-sets amongst the investing public. He adds: "Some say if you don't give guidance, people will come up with their own conclusions and it will add volatility. But I don't think company guidance on First Call has dampened volatility in the market. I think guidance often amplifies volatility in the very short term. I say to those folks [analysts], 'You figure out what the company's earning power is.' We're not going to do your work for you."

On the other side of the Atlantic, Robert Woods of P&O observes that the ability of an analyst to understand a business and to value a business are two different issues. "On the whole," he adds, "I would describe their level of under-standing of our business as slight. I would like to put half of these analysts that we talk to into trying to run a big business like ours. I would very much like to see them having a go." On the other hand, he notes: "They're not stupid. They don't understand what goes into running a business with 10,000 employees, trade unions, and the complexities of world trade. But their understanding of the issues that affect our business is not bad. The IQ of a lot of the analysts is high," he adds with humor. "In fact, you could argue that they shouldn't be analysts. They should be running proper businesses."

Sprint's Bob Dellinger notes that there's a difference in companies like Coke getting out of the earnings guidance process and companies with other business models. "Coke," he says, "sells billions of bottles every month and they're prob-ably predictable within a fraction of a percent. If the economy goes up, they're probably going to grow a little bit faster. If the economy goes down, they'll probably grow a little bit slower. They're not going to surprise analysts because of some fundamental thing."

In determining whether to give earnings guidance, Dellinger says companies need to consider the predictability of their business model. For example, he says: "Our business is a little tougher to predict. We're in multiple product lines. We're making strategic changes. And in the absence of information from the company to analysts, those analysts will create their own models. And we expect them to create their models. We provide annual financial guidance as one data point to help analysts in creating valuation models, not to drive the answer, but to provide our best thinking regarding our financial expectations and targets. Arguably, without any insight or guidance from us, they're going to create a broader range of answers. And some of them, we know, are going to be pessimistic or optimistic. Now, an investor can choose one of the analysts. They can choose our guidance, or they can choose to come up with their own. At least we've provided our annual financial expectations."

DEFINING FINANCIAL TRANSPARENCY:

In March 2002, John Morrissey, Deputy Chief Accountant of the SEC, offered the U.S. House of Representatives Subcommittee on Oversight and Investigations this definition: "A primary goal of the federal securities laws is to promote honest and efficient markets and informed investment decisions through full and fair disclosure. Transparency in financial reporting, that is, the extent to which financial information about a company is available and understandable to investors and other market participants, plays a fundamental role in making our markets the most efficient, liquid, and resilient in the world."

Transparency and analyst guidance are fundamentally about nurturing a relationship with the investor. Healthy relationships involve discernment, candor where necessary, and openness where it aids an investor's ability to put data in context and make judgments accordingly. We are all investors in one facet of our lives or another, so at some level, using our own sensibilities as an aid, the choice of how and what information to share becomes not all that unclear.

CONCLUSION

Financial risk management is probably the most mature component of the larger enterprise or strategic risk management process. C-level executives and treasury departments in particular have a wealth of both history and tools to shield their primary financial assets from undue and unwanted volatility. Because of this, shareholders will have more limited tolerance for financial missteps. Instituting a sound financial risk program is the first line of tactical defense. Implemented properly, it should have a significant value added, not least through new business that would have been refused without the risk management techniques now available.

CHAPTER 6

The Enemy Within— Responding to Operational Risk

"We have met the enemy and he is us."

—Pogo (Walt Kelly)

The events that brought down Barings Bank and Enron were not instances of market or credit or operations risk. These were situations where companies suffered huge monetary losses because of inadequate or faulty internal processes, people, or systems. And this is precisely the definition for operational risk proposed by the Basel Committee on Banking Supervision (BCBS).[1]

In some ways, the term "operational risk" is a catchall for risks that do not fit into discrete risk categories. There are no large databases of historical results that lend themselves to economic modeling and statistical analysis of operational risks. On the other hand, these do exist for market and credit risk, and we've been far more successful in modeling, monitoring, and managing their systemic proclivities.

Interestingly, as we described in *Security Transformation,* minor changes in internal controls can have a big impact on risk. For example, just by using better passwords, network security can be bolstered as much or more than by installing millions of dollars of security detection devices. Similarly, many of the operational risks—such as rogue trading at Barings and Daiwa (discussed later in this chapter)—that played havoc with companies, shareholders, stakeholders, and pension funds might have been thwarted by better internal controls.

The BCBS definition also includes external events, and, clearly, the losses of personnel and records suffered by Cantor-Fitzgerald in the wake of the World Trade Center attacks are not flawed internal systems or people. But if companies can reduce the opportunity for internal operational-risk events, they can qualitatively reduce at least the probabilities, and perhaps the severity, of such events

In the absence of models and meaningful statistics for low-frequency/high-severity events, we must again turn to what we can control and try to limit the potential damage from what we cannot. At that same time, we need to take a fresh look at these events to see if the application of processes like total quality management (TQM) can reduce those risks before we apply risk management strategies. For example, by improving the accuracy of phoned-in catalog sales orders, the costs of repeat handling and shipping may be reduced enough to require no risk management intervention.

A relatively recent idea for improving operational risk management called "near miss" management has its roots in the aviation and chemical industries, where catastrophic events are often preceded by near-miss instances.

A tragic example was the O-ring failure responsible for the 1986 Challenger shuttle disaster; and another, more recent example—the destruction upon reentry of the shuttle Columbia after foam hit the leading edge of the left wing. In both cases post facto investigations indicated prior problems related to the O-ring and dislodged foam. And, as the independent report on Columbia, released in August 2003, stated: "NASA organizational culture had as much to do with the accident as the foam that struck the Orbiter on ascent."[2] It's conceivable that had corrective steps in materials or procedures been taken, the high-severity event might have been prevented.

Near-miss management has been proposed as an additional resource for financial industry operational risks, but it appears to have some relevance for nonfinancial industries as well. It will be discussed in more detail later in the chapter. First, let's examine one case history that speaks emphatically about the need for beefing up internal controls and processes.

DAIWA BANK

In August 1995 the executive vice president of Daiwa Bank's New York branch wrote a 30-page letter to the bank's president in Japan confessing that he had lost about $1.1 billion trading in U.S. Treasury bonds. The trading loss eclipsed that of Barings Bank, but Daiwa had $200 billion in assets and $8 billion in reserve, so if losses were the only problem, the bank could withstand the loss. But they weren't the only problem.[3]

Tashihide Iguchi had been trading the bank's money over an 11-year period and using his position as head of the branch's securities custody department to cover up the losses by selling off securities owned by Daiwa and its customers. In addition to Iguchi's cover-up, senior managers at Daiwa also tried to hide details of the transgressions from July 1995, when Iguchi first confessed, until mid-September, when the loss was finally reported to the U.S. Federal Reserve Board.[4] It was the cover-up, in fact, that led to criminal indictments against the bank and its officers, and to Daiwa—one of Japan's largest commercial banks—being prohibited from doing business in U.S. markets.[5]

Daiwa's New York branch was first opened in the 1950s, and began dealing in U.S. Treasury securities as part of its pension-fund customer services. Iguchi joined the New York branch in 1977, where he soon ran the small back office of its securities business. Promoted to a trader in 1984, Iguchi retained his back-office responsibilities. Moreover, he supervised the securities custody department for about 18 years, right up to 1995.

U.S. Treasury bonds bought by Daiwa, as well as those bought on behalf of customers, were managed by Iguchi's department through a subcustody account with Bankers Trust. Interest was collected and dispersed, and bonds were transferred or sold, based on instructions from customers or Daiwa's managers. Bankers Trust issued transaction reports that flowed through Iguchi's department.

Early on, when losses started to mount, Iguchi authorized sales of bonds and hid the transactions by altering Bankers Trust account statements. And, for 11 years, he falsified account statements and forged more than 30,000 trading slips. But according to investigators, Daiwa's internal auditors never verified either. When customers ordered the sale of bonds Iguchi had already sold, he would sell additional bonds to pay them, and changed more records to cover his tracks. When Iguchi finally revealed his transgressions, he had sold $377 million in customer securities and $733 million in Daiwa holdings to paper over his trading losses.

One needs to put Iguchi's actions in perspective. After the Iguchi affair, further probing by U.S. federal investigators found that the bank had engaged in unauthorized trading between 1986 and 1993, and attempted to hide its activities by temporarily moving traders to different locations and disguising a trading room as a storage room during regulatory visits. Even so, in 1993 regulators chided Daiwa for having traders report to Iguchi as head of the securities custody department.

The bank assured the regulators that it would change that reporting structure, but in fact it did not. In November 1995 the Federal Reserve Board, the New York State Banking Department, and the banking departments of California, Illinois, Massachusetts, Florida, and Georgia issued a joint order terminating the banking operations of Daiwa Bank in the United States. Their statement documented a number of charges, asserting: "The agencies have taken these actions on the basis of information indicating that Daiwa and The Daiwa Bank Trust Company and their officials engaged in a pattern of unsafe and unsound banking practices and violation of law over an extended period of time that are most serious in nature."[6]

By the end of January 1996, Daiwa agreed to sell its U.S. assets and offices, and in February it agreed to pay a $340 million fine. In September 2000 the court in Osaka, Japan, held that some current and former board members, as well as some Daiwa Bank executives, were obligated to pay the bank $775 million in restitution. That action is currently under appeal.

Like Barings Bank, Daiwa had a rogue trader and inadequate separation of duties.

The following requirements would have gone far in mitigating or preventing similar situations:

☐ Separate risk-taking functions from record-keeping and risk-assessment functions

☐ Monitor and respond to earlier warning signals in risk management

☐ Identify and fix errant internal controls

☐ Use effective internal audit procedures focused on risk, including procedures requiring verification of key information with third parties

THOUGHTS ON OPERATIONAL RISK MANAGEMENT

"Personally, I do not see any distinction between good management and good risk management in a world where most important decisions have uncertain outcomes," says Dr. Jacques Pezier.[7]

From a business perspective, operational risk management requires an organizationwide understanding that risks are managed within and around the company's processes, and that they are inextricably linked to the company's business strategy and ability to generate returns. Pattie Dunn believes that the responsibility for operational risk management "lies side by side with a responsibility for returns generation at every level of management, and that at every level of management there should be support for the risk management aspects of their responsibility, just as there is support for the returns generating aspects of their responsibility."

To make the distinction, Dunn says, "I'll describe the opposite, which is much more common. You've got managers who are responsible for the delivery of a product to the market. They are responsible for the operational activities. But the risk in those activities is almost hived off mentally and delegated to people who don't even necessarily report to the managers. These people could be auditors. They could be compliance people. They could be technical people. But they're not really a part of the manager's total responsibility. They're sort of bolted onto the side of the organization, and ultimately, it will not be possible to use risk management to support value creation, which is what risk management needs to be about."

In essence, organizations with fragmented functions and responsibilities, limited and codified communications, preference for *super stars* over *super teams*, unclear objectives, and ethical ambiguities are, says Pezier, organizations "prone to running blindly into operational accidents."

In contrast, companies that are good at expressing their global objectives, encourage internal communication and cooperation, and put checks and balances into decision and control processes are less likely to be blindsided and surprised.

Recognizing that management must make decisions in the context of complex, interrelated, uncertain factors, their schematic should include:

☐ Identifying and framing problems to be addressed

☐ Translating limited information into quantitative probabilities

☐ Expressing risk preferences

SQUARING THE CIRCLE

Practically speaking, a manager will want to chart the frequency and severity of what he or she has identified as their primary operational risks. A simple grid structure, like the one below, works well.

Among the items to be considered and charted is the risk of repetitive losses related to ongoing activities. These could include order entry errors, products shipped that prove faulty, repair costs associated with incoming materials that were not properly quality approved, and so forth. These risks tend to be common in many corporations, though with minimal impact in most. As such, management will weigh the cost of fixing those controls before diving in headlong. In many cases, by improving the quality of service or manufacturing the risk of losses can be significantly mitigated without huge investment.

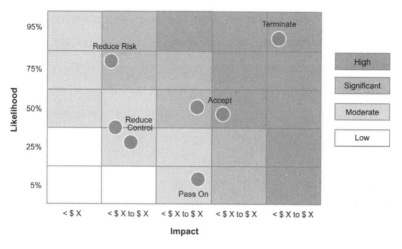

Source: KPMG, 2002

The bulk of senior management time will be spent consulting over the most critical risks—those that pass the "high" threshold despite their frequency. Here, you might discuss the possibility of a SARS quarantine in Singapore impeding delivery of hard-disk drives and the resulting impact on PC production and sales. Here, you would discuss the control loophole that allowed a Barings Bank rogue trader to wreak such havoc, or where you would consider what NASA might have done differently to anticipate the damage during shuttle launches. Here, you can identify and assess probabilities and severities, within the limits of statistical manipulation.

The purpose of such charting is to lead to robust discussion and more effective planning. Until the spate of malicious computer virus activity in 2003, many companies could have thought the task of assessing the impact and likelihood of a virus attack to be an unnecessarily laborious and costly exercise for an "outlier" type risk. We suspect the project has landed on the desks of several managers in several corporations since then. In their review and response, myriad trade-offs will need to be made between security, costs, and convenience. For example, their considerations might include questions such as: Should the system do a virus-detection routine every time a client connects? Must every communication and transaction be backed up and stored remotely, and for how long? What about disaster recovery? How long should it take to fully restore the system?

To be effective, such a project—and any operational risk category with enterprisewide consequences—must have an executive sponsor. Otherwise, the team could easily get caught up in the details while missing the big-picture issues, and also because many risks cross functions and departments. As Pezier describes it, a team of experts without management guidance "would be no better than a patrol of ants trying to make sense of a [Jackson] Pollock painting by running all over it." The executive sponsor will also have the best sense of such soft but vital elements as the impact of a crippling virus on the company's brand and reputation, and will be in the best position to advise on the possible monetary consequences of such damage.

NEAR-MISS OPERATIONAL RISK MANAGEMENT

An interesting paper written by Alexander Muermann, assistant professor of insurance and risk management, the Wharton School, University of Pennsylvania; and Ulku

Oktem, senior fellow at Wharton's Risk Management and Decision Processes Center, deals with near-miss management of operational risk.[8] The article discusses the concept in the context of financial institutions, but it appears to have significance for nonfinancial businesses as well. In fact, the concept, say the authors, is distilled from the chemical and aviation industries.

"In reviewing incidents in process industries, it has been observed that for every major accident there have been a large number of incidents with limited impact and an even larger number of incidents with no damage. Analogously, major operational losses in the banking industry have its predecessors in forms of small abnormalities that do not necessarily cause any losses." The authors point out that sometimes near misses are evidenced by extreme profits rather than losses. In the Barings Bank case, for example, the rogue trader's actions earlier masked the losses and ended up showing much higher than expected gains for arbitrage trading. That was a near miss that could have, and should have, been detected.

The main point is that a near miss clearly presents an opportunity for improvement. The more attuned an organization is to tracking the indicators of unwanted volatility, the more time and maneuverability it gives itself to respond.

Because operational risk is not precisely defined, operational near-misses can be spuriously defined. Identification, therefore, is helped immeasurably if preceded by examples and guidelines. Disclosure has to be both simple and encouraged if it is to be effective. If the near-miss system is working properly, there will be a large number reported, so prioritization and classification are essential for sorting through and deciding where to focus attention.

Near misses that rise to the top of the stack require that the appropriate managers and groups are informed. Thus, organizational prerequisites have to be made to set up such a management approach. Once a near miss is identified and prioritized, its cause(s) must be ferreted out. It is important to distinguish between apparent causes and root causes, and aim for the latter. For example, if a Daiwa auditor had discovered an erroneous trading slip, the apparent cause might have looked administrative but the root cause would have proved to be organizational.

The logical progression is to go from cause to solution. Logically, each cause must be matched to a solution. Each solution must be analyzed to ensure that it doesn't create new problems, and each solution must be linked to a person responsible for its implementation. Once a course of action is prescribed, information about it needs to be disseminated to those involved. And, finally, once implemented, it needs to be evaluated and refined.

CONTINGENCY PLANNING

As those who lived through the massive blackout that darkened the northeastern corner of the United States or the smaller blackout that ground London's Underground to a halt at rush hour know, it's nice to have a backup.

What passes for a typical day usually involves waking up in the morning to find out how the world has shifted overnight.

You may read in the newspapers that employees are threatening to strike at a key supplier. You check messages and find a client wants to move your carefully crafted pitch up two days. You check the overnight reports and find, contrary to forecast, that orders are way up in one part of the business and flat in another. In this fashion the day's order of business is reset. From experience, adaptive organizations understand that much of management's time is invested in the art of contingency planning. When something important changes, how do you respond?

Most leaders understand the fiduciary responsibility to have business continuity plans in place. "If you have an earthquake," says Brent Callinicos of Microsoft, "it isn't just the property. Ask the analyst on Wall Street, 'Do you care if we have a billion dollars in property insurance or not?' What the analyst cares about in the earthquake is not the buildings. They care about whether it will affect the next version of Windows." This is true for all companies, regardless of product or service.

Reality and common sense dictate that the most important contingency plans are those that cover the most important assets. What are sometimes overlooked, however, are the operational nodes that allow those assets to function as planned. While some of these might leap out, like a critical parts supplier, others can seem banal, easily substituted and not worth worrying about. Test some of those assumptions.

Before taking over the helm of British Airways, Rod Eddington worked for Cathay Pacific for many years and was based in Hong Kong. Early in the 1990s someone robbed a jewelry store close to the old Kai Tak airport. The robber, pursued by the police, took to his heels, and fled into the airport area, where he happened to spy the Cathay Pacific flight kitchen and leaped inside. The police instantly cordoned off the flight kitchen and no one was allowed in or out. This of course meant no meals could get in or out. "Now," Eddington says, "you would happily dispatch an airplane to Taipei without a meal, because it is a one hour flight, and you could apologize to customers." Even a two and a half hour flight, "from Hong Kong to Bangkok, you could dispatch without meals." But, he adds, "Would you send a 14-hour flight to London from Hong Kong without any meals at all? Who would have ever thought the airline could be brought to a halt by a robber ending up in the flight kitchen? Not in a million years would you have foreseen that." But he concludes: "We could and should have foreseen the possibility of the flight kitchen being inoperative, and had contingency plans for that."

Eddington believes that today, companies are thinking about and taking business continuity plans in a different and better direction. "People are realizing that business continuity is at risk in a whole range of ways that would normally not have been heard about, something that's particularly true in our just-in-time world. There is a whole range of things that could prevent an airline from running properly," he adds, "And you need to try to think through the business continuity issues of failure at any point in the chain, and then work out what you can do to mitigate that."

This has been Jeff Clarke's lifeblood for the last year or so. As HP's head of global operations, Clarke knows there is enormous risk when you're running some $50 billion of procurement across the supply chain. If there are vulnerabilities in the chain, he wants to know about them, and fast. "Are there external events," he asks his team, "be it wars, the SARS epidemic, or others, that could impact our logistics flows?" (At the time we spoke to Clarke, a hurricane was heading toward Houston, home of one of HP's major factories.)

If so, Clarke can draw on a number of tools to help. "Our supply chain today," he says, "is more mathematical and quantitative than it's ever been, and it requires extraordinary investments in enterprise resource systems, and manufacturing resource planning systems, as well as an intense linkage from supplier to customer." As a large multinational, Hewlett-Packard generates $200 million a day in revenue, which means "literally hundreds of millions of supplies and components."

Accordingly, HP's supply chain has "enormous touch-points and node connections." Given that, Clarke says, "as we step back and try to assess the associated risks, the importance of redundancy and contingency planning becomes clear. It follows that HP has adopted a policy of developing a number of strategic vendors per area of supply, thereby avoiding the inherent risk of single source suppliers." In practice this means that HP maintains nonexclusive relationships with a number of carrier networks, including Federal Express, UPS, and DHL, container ships, and others.

"We build redundancy in through that way," Clarke adds. And just as HP develops purposely redundant IT systems, Clarke expects his supply base to do the same. In fact, a recent trip Clarke made to DHL's data center showed the company to be in the middle of implementing a three-way redundant data center with full fail-over capability so that even if two full data centers went down, DHL could go to a third data center with global reach. It was, Clarke says, "an extraordinary example of an adaptive enterprise." He adds: "We expect our suppliers to have incorporated the notion of IT redundancy into their model because real-time information is critical to us and we cannot afford any failures."

When it comes to modeling the risk of loss or failure, Clarke states: "On the most sophisticated side of the spectrum, we work with our suppliers to build in options within the contract which ensure security of supply, and have penalties for failure to meet that supply."

In so doing, Hewlett-Packard is able to use its size to negotiate strong and favorable contracts. "So let's say for instance that demand is 30 percent higher than expected," Clarke explains. "We will put an option in place in some of our contracts that requires components to come to us first rather than other parts of the market. Being as large a customer as we are, we have the leverage to do that at a different cost level. So when we go out and negotiate our relationships with our vast supply base, it's not just about price; it's also about security of supply. It's about risk management. It's about the ability of our suppliers to flex their upside and their downside with us." He concludes: "We don't want to be caught with a sudden downturn. We want to share that risk, and that goes into the negotiations."

Contingency planning is about protecting the vital nodes in a company's processes, be they operational, financial, or compliance. Your shareholders, the market, and the public expect you to have the backup capability to continue developing and producing if something catastrophic were to occur. Insurance is protection, but it is not a contingency. Among other unpleasantness, without proper backup planning, your company could find itself the defendant in a shareholder lawsuit.

MOVING FORWARD

Operational risk is the least well defined of risks. It is least adaptable to large scale data analysis and modeling, and most difficult to manage rigorously. Yet, consider the damage to shareholder value and investor confidence that can be attributed to operational "incidents" in just the last three years.

As first steps for improving how one deals with operational risks we recommend the following:

☐ Recognize that there's a profound risk of loss caused by deficiencies in information systems, business processes, or internal controls.

☐ Examine your internal controls and map what must be done, internally, to deliver on your business strategy and agreed stakeholder promises, pinpointing organizational obstacles and crafting practical workarounds.

☐ Focus on the handoff points because in any end-to-end process these are likely to be the primary trouble spots.

☐ Ensure that risk factors are embedded in quality programs and organizational education.

Governing Principles

CHAPTER 7

We the People of the Board

> " *It is reason, principle, conscience, the inhabi-*
> *tant of the breast, the man within, the great*
> *judge and arbiter of our conduct . . . who shows*
> *us the propriety of generosity, of reining in the*
> *greatest interests of our own for yet the greater*
> *interests of others, the love of what is honorable*
> *and noble, of the grandeur, and dignity of our*
> *own character.* "
>
> —Adam Smith, proponent of free-market principles and
> author of *The Wealth of Nations*

W ho among us has not felt some sting of shame, some prickle of irritation, at the collective tarnishing of boardroom reputations? Is it true that "our market system has experienced a failure of character," as John Bogle, founder and former CEO of the Vanguard Group, believes? Shouldn't corporate governance be an implicit expectation, much like good character, a set of principles that are simply inherent and understood?

Some of the discomfort with our present situation is that we are forced into a position in which we can no longer say yes categorically. Events have proven otherwise. And although the problems have been made most dramatically manifest by the "few bad apples," disquieting for many of us is the recognition that there were and are things about the governance process, sensible oversight practices, we should have known and observed but didn't, or were too complacent in carrying out.

The last 20 years saw the rise in exotic derivatives, complex off-balance sheet accounting and partnerships. Yet, however intricate and opaque these practices may have become, for those companies and boards who lost sight of the basics, not even the most exquisitely designed hedge could protect them from that more fundamental exposure. The breakdown in the basics, thoughtful scrutiny, meaningful dialogue, frank questioning, careful planning, and candid probing, has emerged as cumulative factors in what has become a fundamental failure in oversight.

Jay Keyworth, a member of Hewlett-Packard's board, is widely recognized as an astute observer of corporations and management. These days, risk and governance play on his mind. In his 18 years with HP's board, service as chairman of the Progress & Freedom Foundation, work as Science Adviser to President Reagan, practice as Director of Physics at Los Alamos, and while a member of six different boards, Keyworth has dealt with risk and governance issues from a range of perspectives. When we asked what the requirements of a board member were today, he told us: "We went through a brief period in history believing you could manage and not lead. "And we're past that. You can't manage without leading. And if you're going to lead, you have to know about business risk areas, and board members have to be part of that process. It's a return to a leadership model."

Simply stated, you have to know your business: what it does, where it comes from, where it's going, and what can hobble it along the way. "In my years at HP and in talking to other board members from large Fortune 50 companies," Keyworth notes, "I find that people thought that actually becoming familiar with the business itself and the details of the business, and particularly the half-dozen major areas of potential risk the company faces, was not really a board responsibility."

We all point to Enron as a collective example of people who did not uphold their responsibility. And there's no question that happened. But Keyworth thinks it's too easy to cast a broad brush across Enron. "Enron is an interesting story," he says. "There's a company that was young and had grown very, very rapidly, but most of all it was a company that was in a whole new set of business areas where there weren't good models and their business practices were very rapidly evolving and, you know, if you really look carefully, they did not have a bad board. They had some very good people on that board. I knew some of those folks, and some of them were very conscientious people. But, nevertheless, in the aftermath it is very, very clear that there was not a sense on that board that they needed to be aware of the details of the business."

It wasn't that they did not understand the intricate financing arrangements, nearly doctoral in their complexity.

They didn't. But the more fundamental problem, says Keyworth, was that "they felt they did not need to really come to grips with the competitive forces in the industry, the areas of fundamental change." In Enron's case, that fundamental change was the basic underlying shift in the regulatory environment, and the market's and Enron's response. They didn't focus on that, and the rest of the web unraveled around them.

STRATEGIC RISK OVERSIGHT

Turning to the board's fundamental role, then, we'll discuss four key steps to strategic risk oversight.

Step One: What Are the Risks?

If boards were in any doubt about their overarching responsibility to let risk drive their review, this quotation from the November 2002 *Report of the National Association of Corporate Directors Blue Ribbon Commission on Risk Oversight* clarifies any residual ambiguity:

This board's role, quite simply, is to provide risk oversight. This means making sure that management has instituted processes to identify, and bring to the board's attention, the major risks the enterprise faces. It also means the continual reevaluation of these monitoring processes and the risks with the help of the board and its committees.

In considering this responsibility, ask yourself, do you understand the half-dozen or so major risks that lie before your company? At least annually, schedule time for board and management to identify these items together:

- ☐ Top stakeholder interests

- ☐ Top strategic initiatives

- ☐ The primary financial, operational, regulatory risks that could imperil them

- ☐ The means by which you will define and communicate to senior management the board's tolerance for risks, and how you intend to match that risk tolerance against the company's strategies

In tandem with this exercise, discuss and determine how much risk you are currently exposed to and how much you wish to carry. As a board member, are you comfortable with how well you understand your company's risk profile and risk culture?

Some companies are likely to be less risk tolerant than others; a pension fund management company versus a venture capital management firm, for example. While clarifying and accepting a company's risk stance is the CEO's job, support, oversight, and acceptance from the board are essential. "Without such guidance," states a McKinsey survey, "a company's risk strategy will be made—and repeatedly redefined accidentally—by dozens of everyday financial and business decisions."[1]

That risk oversight responsibility is something that Mark Hurd, CEO of NCR, takes very seriously. "We try to do a risk analysis on every strategic decision that we make," he says.

"We've got a risk process that we do at the board level. And we try to look at risk relative to competition, to customers, and to internal factors. Typically in each of our businesses, three potential problems have to be considered. Either the market could change or our competitive position could change, or there's some internal obstacle that we might have to overcome. Those are the risks we look at."

Step Two: Focus on Areas of Change

Boardrooms are nice places to work, accoutered as they are with attractive tables, pleasant lighting, and intelligent people. Yet, they are no places to test strategy. For that, one must go outside. During the United States war with Iraq, Secretary of Defense Donald Rumsfeld repeatedly reminded us that "no war plan survives first contact with the enemy." And, as history has shown as far back as Sun Tzu's *Art of War*, even the most pacifist among us can draw business lessons from military doctrine. Top boards study their competitors and other businesses, not only within their own sector, but across industry lines.

This is more urgent now than ever before. A surprising thing has happened over the last generation. As government-owned businesses have given way to private enterprise, barriers to entry have crumbled. The competitive landscape has morphed and grown to a point few companies would have imagined. Nontraditional sectors have sprung into traditional paths and are nibbling away at market share. Five years ago who would have listed Wal-Mart laundry detergent as the number one competitive threat to Proctor & Gamble's Tide?

Probably very few. Not even P&G, despite that company's legendary prowess at industry benchmarking, spotted it. Yet, today, Wal-Mart's laundry detergent is forcing P&G to significantly rethink its strategy to defend its major powerhouse brand.

Keyworth calls this "dynamic competition." It's not merely the presence of more or surprising new competitors. It's the speed. "You get more competition. You get more speed, and this creates enormous risks," he stresses.

Indeed, Keyworth notes that when a Stanford business professor gave a talk to some members of HP's audit committee, he commented that the board "must focus on areas of change," change in the marketplace, change inside the company, anything, in fact, that is new. And they must give these new areas a very high level of scrutiny and sensitivity.

Step Three: Test and Benchmark

A major component of the board's strategic oversight role is to ensure that good benchmarking and very good competitor intelligence are crafted. Friends at IBM, a major HP competitor, frequently tell Keyworth: "Jay, we know more about HP than you do." But by the same token, Keyworth adds, "I certainly hope we know a lot about IBM, and, of course, we do."

Likewise, British Airways CEO Rod Eddington recognizes he is responsible for leading a business that is in the midst of swirling change and massive consolidation. He knows the survivors will be the ones with their ears to the ground. As a consequence, he is constantly asking himself what lessons those who work in the airline industry can take from other industries, whether they're manufacturing, consumer products, or financial services industries. "Because," he says, "many of the risks that we face, they face, albeit in slightly different forms, and we need to be smart about how we recognize that and what lessons we can learn from them." He adds: "You know better than I do that this issue of risk, risk assessment, risk mitigation, and risk management is something that most sensible companies take very seriously now. And if they don't, things like the Barings problem in Singapore is sort of a wakeup call to everybody. And I think your first instinct when something like that happens is to say, 'Could that happen in my company? What have we done in my company, or at our company, to mitigate against the possibility of that risk?'"

Benchmarking should ideally represent the combination of both informal and formal processes. Board members can use outside groups to conduct formal studies and analyses, but these need to be compared and updated against media reports, analyst statements, and investor comments. They need to challenge CEOs and ask them: How does your approach to the given risk or opportunity differ from the way the CEO of your competitor is handling it, and why is your way better, and what circumstances will most impact your considerations?

In addition, the strategy being developed should be pulled out at every board meeting and tested and retested, along with a major board review annually, to satisfy all parties that the approach is sound, vetted, and the optimal means of meeting their and their stakeholders' goals.

Step Four: Recognize the Interrelationship of Risks

"When an aircraft crashes," says Eddington, "it's usually three or four things going wrong sequentially or simultaneously, and often if you had been able to prevent one of those three or four things going wrong, you would have prevented the accident itself."

As the board reviews the primary risk set that management has drawn up, they need to ask management about risk interactions and ensure that the right controls are in place to respond to the most serious. If a company is planning on expanding its operations in continental Europe, for example, will that shift in employee base increase the company's strike risk? Given Europe's strong labor laws, will it impair the company's ability to streamline operations in the event of falling fortunes? Would the impact of those events create a material event that the company would then have to disclose? The answer may well be no, but it is a crucial element of a board member's fiduciary responsibility to discover and understand the answer.

STEWARDSHIP

While a board's strategic risk oversight may involve the preceding four steps, for the steps to occur, governance practices must establish the conditions that allow them to take place. This involves culture, communication, and commitment coming together under the mantle of stewardship.

As a steward, a director's reach extends to the management of risk, shareholder communications, legal and regulatory compliance, and the audit and financial risk management process. The influence of such stewardship is evident in organizational ethics, company reputation, and the loyalty of investors, customers, suppliers, and employees. Its quality, good or bad, can change how much an organization pays to borrow money; determine the quality of an organization's vendors, partners, and employees; affect what premium investors will pay for an organization's shares; and influence an organization's reputation in the marketplace.[2] By virtue of all of this, governance and value are inextricably tied.

What type of environment should boards strive for in fulfilling their role as risk overseers? Let's start with culture.

Culture

The board sets the "tone at the top," which is to say they assert the character of the organization. If one were to go around a boardroom and ask each director to describe the character of the company they serve, odds are, an equal number of descriptions would emerge. This is because character and culture are subjective, each colored by perspective and experience. Chances are equally good, however, that at the center of most descriptions would be words like integrity, accountability, decency, quality, customer service, words that comprise most companies' set of core values, the corporate canon of ethics.

If anyone remains ignorant of the importance such values play, they have been away a long time. The ramifications on brand, reputation, and stock price when unethical or negligent behavior has defiled a company's governance principles are well known. Recovery in these cases is not impossible, but it is burdensome. Shareholders become twice shy, performance becomes impaired, scrutiny intensifies, and trusted relationships often break down. Suffice it to say, culture matters, and sincere efforts to ensure ethical conduct are part of the cloth of governance.

THE RELATIONSHIP BETWEEN CULTURE AND FRAUD

The International Standard on Auditing 240: Responsibility of Those Charged with Governance and of Management, states, "The primary responsibility for the prevention and detection of fraud and error rests with both those charged with the governance and the management of an entity. The respective responsibilities of those charged with governance and management may vary by entity and from country to country. Management, with the oversight of those charged with governance, needs to set the proper tone, create and maintain a culture of honesty and high ethics, and establish appropriate controls to prevent and detect fraud and error within the entity."

Viacom CFO Richard Bressler sees this as a crucial factor: "We have a tone, set at the top of the house, that is extremely open. We take nothing for granted. We invite people to communicate right to the top on any news, without repercussions whatsoever. And we go to great lengths to ensure that there are never any repercussions. If there is something, an internal control issue, or a fraud issue, or an ethics issue, we invite them to come in and talk about it. And I think we handle those things in a way that creates an environment that makes it comfortable for people to freely communicate."

Establishing the right "tone" necessarily starts with appointing the right directors. Certainly this means finding candidates who possess excellent qualifications. But increasingly it also means finding candidates who match the company's personality, values, culture, and need for independence. The Germans have a term called "gestalt" that they use to describe a structure or experience that manifests greatness only when all component parts are added together. In fact, a whole school of psychology has sprung up around it. Gestalt psychology looks for the larger contribution and understanding that come from the successful and complete interaction of many things acting in concord together.

In many ways, it's this spirit one should be assessing when evaluating candidates for board membership. How will the prospect add to the discussion? Will he or she energize debate, offer collegiality, and bring forth their own personality and commitment? These considerations form the basis of one's approach. As the makeup of the boardroom shifts from the country club atmosphere that characterized many boardrooms during earlier decades, the best will be marked by spirited interest and deep intellectual curiosity.

The Stanford Directors College runs a session it calls, "How to Ask Questions and Challenge Management Without Creating a Riot." This gets to the nub of the culture issue. Just as our chapter on audit committees discusses the fine line between oversight and management, many directors struggle to find the right balance between criticism and collegiality. Yet boards have to challenge management. This does not mean they need to be combative or stubbornly evangelize an effort to the detriment of the company. It does, however, mean pushing back again, and again, and again. An independent voice is an important facet of what it means to fulfill the independence requirement of a board member's fiduciary responsibility.

The third element of a board's culture-setting mandate is permeating the notion throughout the company that risk management is everybody's responsibility, from the chairman and CEO right down to the line employee. BA's Eddington is adamant about this point: "People further down the organization can often identify risks and articulate them in a way that others cannot see. Risks to our business are often identified not by the people who sit in the senior offices, but from a range of levels in the business." Good boards take advantage of this intelligence pool by cultivating an open culture where avenues for risk discussions are easily available.

To aid boards in reviewing their corporate culture and values, an undeniably soft topic, here are three items to consider:

☐ Establish a system of values supported by a code of conduct that stipulates both acceptable and unacceptable employee behavior.

☐ Establish procedures, including communication and training, to help ensure understanding and ownership of organizational values and the code of conduct by management and all employees.

☐ Use organizational values to drive business value and competitive advantage.

Management Compensation

The compensation of management is clearly an important component in setting the right tone at the top. How much should a good CEO get paid? What percentage of the compensation package will be in the form of stock options or grants? What retirement package will the CEO receive? These are a few of the issues compensation committees of the board are dealing with today.

Management compensation has been in the spotlight for the last several years, sparked by the high-profile corporate collapses of 2001 and 2002. Investors, absorbing the pains of a recessionary economy, have little tolerance for executive pay packages that seem wildly disproportionate to the company's performance or lack thereof.

The September 2003 departure of Dick Grasso, former chairman of the New York Stock Exchange (NYSE), over a pay package that topped $140 million, is a striking indication of how public sentiment has evolved. What makes Grasso's departure striking is that it may go on record as the first time a man widely acknowledged as having done a superb job was made to step down over the size of his paycheck.

Given the prestige of the NYSE and the attention the matter has received, there is little doubt that the event will have far reaching consequences. Certainly there will be more pressure on compensation committees to operate with a greater degree of scrutiny and restraint. Indeed, as Viacom CFO Richard Bressler notes, the management and compensation committees of most companies will "absolutely have it in the back of their mind in terms of risk, in terms of the relationship with shareholders, and in terms of what they think is an appropriate amount to pay you."

From a risk management perspective, senior management compensation with inappropriately structured incentives can be a problem. One of the clearly defined risks of fraudulent financial reporting comes from the incentive or pressure that individuals with significant financial interests in a company may have to commit financial reporting fraud. Indeed, formal fraud risk assessment standards, such as those presented in the Statement on Auditing Standards 99 (SAS 99), state that there are three conditions that allow fraud to occur: incentives and/or pressure, opportunities, and attitudes (e.g., lack of integrity). Good corporate governance can help address all three.

For one thing, boards will certainly recognize that compensation is increasingly a public matter—not least because of Sarbanes-Oxley and Nasdaq/NYSE proposals to that effect.

In light of these changes, compensation committees need to review their charters and their roles. In many cases a much higher independence standard will need to be maintained.

Among the questions committee members should ask:[3]

1. Should members be selected by nominating or governance committees?

2. Do the compensation committee members have adequate access to and control over the outside compensation consultants?

3. Are bonus programs structured to enhance long-term stockholder value?

4. How does the compensation committee measure executive performance?

5. Are the criteria tied to value creation and building? What role should nonfinancial criteria play in the measurement?

6. Are committee members able to effectively negotiate with the CEO over compensation?

7. Is there a mechanism that could enable the company to recover payments to executives who engage in improper conduct?

8. Does equity compensation align management's interests with the stockholders' interests?

9. Should executives be required to hold stock until after retirement?

10. How does the committee measure total compensation (i.e., salary, bonus, equity incentives, perquisites)?

Such items all play a role in shaping an executive's motivations.

Communication

Edward R. Murrow once said: "Anyone who isn't confused doesn't really understand the situation." Business is not simple. It never was, and it has become several orders of magnitude more complex today. For effective risk oversight, boards need to step up the quality of communication between themselves and management as well as between the company and its investors, analysts, and other important constituents.

Board and Management Communications

The proper symbiosis between management and directors occurs through meaningful contact. While the old proverb warns about familiarity breeding contempt, for boards it breeds valuable knowledge. In fact, the best symbioses are characterized by close working relationships between a director and a manager. These are relationships that each side works hard to cultivate, wherein either individual can pick up the phone at will to discuss an issue of concern. Managers benefit from collegial, frank, and private discussions with an experienced "sounding board," someone who will tell it to them as it is. Board members, for their part, who are necessarily more removed from day-to-day operations, acquire from management sharper insights, a sense of what's keeping the manager "up at night," and a more defined grasp of where the risks and opportunities lie.

The benefits from actively nurtured (as opposed to "chummy") relationships spill over into the board meetings themselves, where higher levels of engagement between board and management aid true and open exchange. The respective parties, less hidebound by the polite strains of acquaintanceship, are simply freer to rouse robust, intelligent, constructive discussion, exactly the type needed to refine strategy and risks most thoughtfully.

Moving this to a more formal plane, one emerging best practice observed from our interviews and research is the establishment of an annual off-site between boards and top managers to discuss strategy, risk, and oversight. In addition to the board and executive management, the gathering should include the company's key risk managers, including its chief risk officer, head of internal audit, chief information officer, and other pertinent figures who reflect the full spectrum of business and risk conditions impacting the company.

This gathering should be supplemented:

☐ Midyear, through a follow-on off-site or extended board meeting styled to allow for any mid-course corrections that may be required

☐ With a self-evaluation by management of its strategic risk management processes, as well as an evaluation of these processes by the board

☐ With a self-evaluation of the board's oversight of strategic risk management processes and an evaluation by management of this oversight

Like many of the executives we spoke with, Sprint CFO Bob Dellinger supports the idea of having an annual risk review with the board. While Dellinger is fervent that managers need to make a habit of periodic operating reviews with their business units, he acknowledges that it "can be hard to get up to the really big issues in those kinds of discussions." But with boards, you can do that. He states: "With boards, you can talk about the fundamental changes in the industry, fundamental changes in consumer demand. You can ask questions like, 'What if local telephony over utility lines works? How would we respond?' So, management and the board can discuss risks and an array of responses." The point, Dellinger says, is not to solve all the risks, but to come away thinking about them, to come away with the blinders off.

For those boards considering such a retreat, the recommended objectives are typically to:

☐ Ensure alignment of goals, strategies, initiatives, and performance measurement systems throughout the organization

☐ Evaluate risks to strategy, and conduct scenario planning

☐ Ensure the organization can deliver against its strategy even as it adapts to evolving circumstances

☐ Assess the risk management processes and underlying infrastructure

Prior to and after this annual gathering, the board may allocate budget and resources to engage specialized advisers to review the strategy and risks identified. The object would be to confirm or extend the board's understanding of management's presentation and any outside factors they may not have considered. The board, in turn, would communicate any new findings with management either at the annual off-site or during a regular, scheduled board meeting.

Ken West, former CEO of Harris Bankcorp and member of Motorola's Audit Committee, says: "There's a natural resistance on the part of management to having outsiders messing around with their boards. Boards either think they don't have the time or the inclination or don't need that kind of consulting." But the reality is that many do.

Many very good and tailored board governance-training programs have sprung up in the wake of the corporate scandals. Both the Stanford Directors' College and the Wharton and the University of Chicago joint venture are among the best in this regard and offer an intensive and targeted education on many of the legal and financial requirements board members need to be aware of and to which they should respond.

Board and Investor Communications

Board interaction with investors is all too frequently limited to formal shareholder gatherings or to semiannual or quarterly analyst briefings. These forums can make it difficult for the ready sharing of thoughts and concerns that top investors need. Some companies, recognizing the important voice of their largest investors, make a point of ensuring that their chairman or other top executives visit personally and regularly with this group to address the company's performance and investor expectations—within the confines of SEC Regulation F.D. (Fair Disclosure).

As Rod Eddington adds: "Suffice it to say if you don't keep the shareholders happy at the end of the day you don't have a business. But you can only keep the shareholders happy in the medium and longer term if you recognize that you free up shareholder value by taking into account the legitimate aspirations of other groups of stakeholders, whether they're employees, communities you serve, customers, or whatever. One of the reasons that having a good risk management structure and processes and mind-set in place is that it helps you improve shareholder value. It gives other stakeholders the confidence that your business is well run."

To that end, for higher quality investor communications, these are among the recommendations we offer boards:

☐ Consult with top stakeholders, such as investors, lenders, customers, and suppliers, when board processes are reviewed, to factor in their interests and concerns.

☐ Review the way in which you communicate governance processes to your shareholders, both institutional and private, and determine whether and how improvements should made.

☐ Ensure that information is concise and timely and that it encompasses appropriate performance measures in keeping with strategic objectives.

Commitment

Effective oversight requires sincere commitment to be independent, knowledgeable, and in attendance. Taking the first, one must nearly go back to New England in 1776 to find a time when the subject of independence received as much passionate championing as today with regard to boards, governance, and the relationship with the external auditor. Still, whatever reforms or restructurings a company considers, none can make up for the basic requirement of qualified, motivated and independent directors who stand for integrity both in their business dealings and in their allegiance to shareholders. At its simplest, the preponderance of a board should be free of any private or business ties with company management so that their opinions, counsel, and judgment will be perceived as unbiased. Such independence should ideally define both the board's leaders and those of its subcommittees. Certainly it should be a prominent feature of nomination committees.

In many European countries the public face of independence is resolved by splitting the roles of chairman and CEO, and appointing a nonexecutive to serve as the former. As with the system of checks and balances inherent in democratic governments, corporations benefit from clearly delineating the management and oversight function. Oracle CFO Jeff Henley believes that in the United States an alternative structure in which "independent lead directors" are appointed will become widespread. "We have several lead directors rather than one chairman who is independent from the CEO," he says, "and that is accepted by the Securities and Exchange Commission. Our three lead directors are paid more than our other directors and do the things that a full-time chairman would do. I think in future you will need to have one or the other, a chairman or lead directors who have the time and independence to represent a check on the CEO."

More companies in the United States are considering switching to one of these approaches. Although human nature is often resistant to power sharing, the more the risk burden is distributed among knowledgeable constituents, the lighter the load and the consequences.

Have You Done Your Homework?

There were always those who regarded appointment to a board as a plum, recognition for past achievements, confirmation of one's social status, and not a great deal of work.

Most of those individuals no longer sit on boards or else have rapidly changed their views. In fact, with today's stringent requirements, some boards may find it difficult to source qualified and interested candidates.

To be up to the task, candidates need to be knowledgeable about the business and the financial measurements used to assess its health and prospects. They need to understand who the company competes with; what the strengths, weaknesses, opportunities, and threats facing it are; and have a sense of the industry and the company's place within it. If the company is a record chain, for instance, with a well-defined product and market set, it all seems straightforward. But if that company grows up to become Virgin with over 200 separate businesses spanning air travel, music, health clubs, weddings, motorcycles, and soft drinks, then getting a full and complete handle on the company's operations becomes a whole lot more complex.

Arriving at the right balance of knowledge requires the active participation of both board and management. While board members have an obvious requirement to do their homework, many operating issues are so complicated that the board must specify its role in essential functions such as strategy, budgeting, and management review.

Roll Call!

Chances are, most directors are using ink, not lead, these days in marking board and committee meetings on their calendars. Regular attendance has become mandatory, a requirement increasingly etched into board charters. For example, Dow

Chemical is required to report whether any director attended fewer than "75 percent of the sum of the total number of Board meetings and the total number of Board committee meetings that each such respective Director was eligible to attend during the past year." Such strictness seems to work. In 2002, Dow had nine board meetings and 40 formal board committee meetings. In every case, the Dow directors exceeded their attendance threshold. Seven out of 13 had 100 percent attendance at all board and board committee meetings they were eligible to attend.[4]

But while commitment requires attendance, its thrust comes from motivation and the right alignment of interests. Whittled down, it means money. Rather than relying on retainers or pay structures tied to attendance, both of which are still common, proactive boards are moving to performance-based compensation in which directors are required to hold a minimum amount of company stock and in which options are being replaced by grants. For example:

☐ In its 2002 report, the Conference Board's Blue Ribbon Panel on Public Trust and Private Enterprise listed "substantial director and top management stock ownership for extended holding periods" as one of its top reforms.

☐ At Praxair, one of several companies to adopt such rules, the board states that directors "must acquire and hold during their service as a Praxair board member shares of the company's stock equal in value to at least five times the base cash retainer for directors."[5]

☐ At FleetBoston Financial, 50 percent of the director's annual retainer is now paid in common stock units, which Fleet's directors are expected to retain until the end of their service.[6]

This trend is likely to become increasingly widespread.

LINKING GOVERNANCE TO VALUE

Conceptually, we understand that good governance and shareholder value are linked. Quantifying that relationship is another matter. Many studies have been conducted trying to prove the point, but so far there is limited hard data. The area is one of great interest to Pattie Dunn, former CEO of Barclays Global Investors and a member of HP's board. She says a number of academics have tried to structure rigorous studies but found it difficult to do so in relation to governance.

Part of the difficulty, Dunn says, is actually defining what you're trying to measure. Much of the time, the terms themselves are soft: "You end up trying to measure things like corporate bylaws and their impact on returns." She mentions that most activist institutional investors and public pension funds are setting aside "their normal [statistical] standard for the support they require to pursue a particular investment strategy, because they believe that governance should matter, and does matter, and even though they can't point to clear academic or well-structured test results, they'll overlook that."

Ken West, in addition to his board responsibilities, is a special adviser on governance to TIAA/CREF, and widely recognized for his work. He believes there is a linkage between good governance processes and good financial performance, but agrees with Dunn that the linkage is hard to make in tangible terms. In taking the inverse, however, West thinks there is definitely a story: "If you look at every one of the disasters we've had, it's been bad governance coupled with greed and downright crooked management." He asserts that "evidence that there is a clear, proven link between good governance and good financial performance is pretty amorphous, but I think there is unquestionably a correlation between poor or inadequate governance and the potential for trouble."

Directionally, those boards we've spoken with are unanimous about wanting to be "cleaner than clean." They recognize that brand, credibility, and reputation have important Street value, even if indirect. Seen in this light, good governance seems about as good an insurance policy against damage to these vital assets as you can get.

CONCLUSION

The importance of the board's responsibility for governance and risk oversight has become abundantly clear. As a July 2002 McKinsey study confirmed, pension fund managers in the United States are willing to pay a premium of up to 14 percent for the shares of organizations that demonstrate good corporate governance practices.[7] Governance pertains to value every bit as much as it pertains to values. And it is ultimately for managing the risks inherent in that equation that board members are called to be both stewards and strategists.

···

CHAPTER 8

The Audit Committee, Risk and Regulation

"Some days even my lucky rocketship under-pants don't help."

—Calvin, American comic strip icon

An audit committee member could be excused for feeling like Sisyphus these days, straining to push a giant boulder up a mountain while vainly hoping to prevent its weight from rolling back down on top of him. Supplant the boulder for piles of paperwork and reams of regulations and suddenly one can feel what it's like to be in those worn leather sandals dug hard against the cliffside. In this second of two chapters devoted to governance issues, we'll look at the role of the audit committee, its responsibilities, and the complex regulations surrounding its position, in a bid to make its weight easier to carry.

KPMG created its Audit Committee Institute (ACI) in 1999 to help audit committee members and senior management respond to the challenges they face. Since then, we have worked with literally thousands of directors, audit committee chairs, and senior management figures to discuss issues and enhance awareness of effective audit committee processes.

THE ROLE AUDIT COMMITTEES PLAY

As a guardian of investor interests and corporate accountability, audit committees have borne the brunt of regulatory and investor scrutiny. Under the glint of this microscope, their role has increasingly been vested with driving risk concerns through the audit committee process, agenda, and framework. A comprehensive consensus view of the oversight responsibilities of the committee—beyond the independence and expertise requirements of current regulations—would benefit the larger discussion on audit committees, so let us begin there.

Whereas historically the work of an audit committee evolved in response to changes in the business environment with little specificity and few mandates, recent reforms and regulations, including the Sarbanes-Oxley Act of 2002, have abruptly formalized the natural evolution of this institution. Thanks to that act and its 130 pages, we now have our first *legal* definition of an audit committee (emphasis added):

A Committee (or equivalent body) established by and amongst the board of directors of an issuer for the purpose of overseeing the accounting and financial reporting processes of the issuer; and audits of the financial statements of the issuer.

In the charged environment that has sprung up in the wake of the corporate scandals, committee members must keep up with what seems an ever-changing rulebook. The complexities of the current environment raise the potential for audit committees to become unduly focused on compliance. Process can overwhelm principle. As audit committees strive hard to watch the referee, they're often hard pressed to pull their gaze back to the game taking place on the field. Directors at the KPMG spring 2003 audit committee roundtables expressed the flavor of some of these concerns:

☐ "Simply complying with all of the new rules takes up considerable audit committee time and can serve as a distraction from its central responsibilities."

☐ "There is a fine line that distinguishes 'oversight' from 'micromanagement.' Where is that line? In a potential lawsuit, someone is likely to say, 'Why didn't you know this or that detail?' How much must we know?"

☐ "It's important to balance practicality and priorities with the new governance environment to ensure that we not only focus on the form [of the various requirements], but also the substance."

☐ "There are too many pronouncements leading to too much checking off of requirements and not enough thinking."

☐ "It's hard to keep up with all the changes in NYSE and SEC reporting and rules, while trying to keep focused on substance rather than details."

In response to these concerns, we have developed a framework for effective risk oversight, a handrail, as it were, that audit committees can use to clamber up from the pool of risks, regulations, and requirements in which they have been submerged. Its goal is to help directors better visualize the primary considerations that lie before them while also giving them a place to start.

Underlying the framework is a core set of questions:

☐ What are the most important risks related to the accounting and financial reporting processes for us to focus on? (See Chapter 7, *We the People of the Board.*)

☐ What type and level of information should management be presenting to the audit committee?

☐ What is the desired level of coordination between the audit committee, management, and the internal and external auditors?

☐ How can we design the committee's processes to make the most effective and efficient use of our time?

☐ How do we stay in compliance with emerging regulations while still maintaining an effective focus on the business?

Reducing it to one line, the essence simply is: how to obtain the right information, from the right party, in the right context, at the right time.

Creating a meaningful risk-based framework is an investment, and a time-consuming one at that. It requires proper information flows—and where flows are inadequate, it needs analysis of where and how improvements should be made. It

A FRAMEWORK FOR EFFECTIVE AUDIT COMMITTEE OVERSIGHT

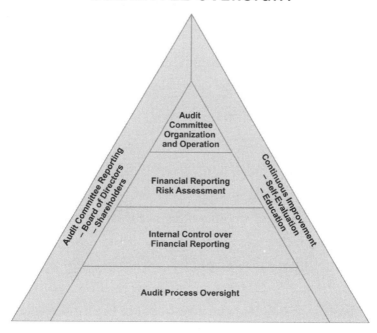

requires thoughtful, open, and candid discussion with the CEO, other members of operations management, CFO, corporate secretary, general counsel, and both the external and internal auditor. And it requires that committee members think deeply about the creation of processes that support their understanding and monitoring of the following:

1. The unique oversight role of the audit committee in relation to the specific roles of the other participants in the financial reporting process, including internal processes to ensure fair, accurate, and complete reporting and disclosure, compliance with regulatory requirements, and communications with the investing public

2. Critical financial reporting risks

3. The effectiveness of the financial reporting process and underlying controls

4. The independence, accountability, and effectiveness of the committee and the external and internal auditors

5. Financial reporting transparency

The French painter Edgar Degas once complained, "I really have a lot of stuff in my head; if only there were insurance companies for that as there are for so many other things." Since there are not, and since we are at a time when audit committee members are grappling with increased responsibilities, a meaningful framework has shown itself to be worth the effort. Most committees with effective processes in place are grateful for the investment of time and recognize the process as a valuable element in protecting their companies and themselves from undue risk exposure.

Before stepping into the framework, we first offer some comments on the overarching principle of oversight.

OVERSIGHT

The line between oversight and management is an admittedly fine one, and audit committee members are often perplexed about how best to tread it. Indeed, micromanage, and one risks the inverse of Dale Carnegie's teaching, with lost friends and alienated people for company. Oversight is about making sure, in the event of a wound, a manager has thought about Band-Aids, has the necessary quantity in stock, and has the skills to apply them. It does not mean having board members roll up their own sleeves to lay on the gauze. Fundamentally, for many it is about refining one's questioning skills.

At an elementary level, the directors we spoke with suggest that rather than asking how a manager is responding to something, focus on *who* is responding and *what* the response consists of. If you're on the board of an electric utility, for example, you don't need to be an engineer to know if the right resources and processes are in place to provide good service to the community. From an oversight perspective, you need to make sure you understand the organizational accountabilities of the *who* in each situation. As Tom Horton, retired chairman of the National Association of Corporate Directors, put it: "Keep your noses in, and your fingers out."

The reality for many committees, however, is that for the "noses" to do their jobs properly, they need to be "in" a whole lot more than they are at present. Jay Keyworth says: "I think there has to be a dialogue between board members and the CEO and board members and the people who are running businesses that says, 'Don't tell me about your business. Tell me about the key areas of risk.'"

Raymond Troubh is the current chairman of the board at Enron. With regard to oversight, he says: "Directors have always had the power; the laws regarding directors have not changed. They are just utilizing the power they already had."[1] This needs to continue. When audit committees have individual business units that are reporting on their businesses from a financial perspective, audit committees need to ask: Where are you most likely to fail?

The directors we spoke to emphasize that audit committee members have to learn how to demand some control of the agenda. They should set the agenda and ask for CFO and auditor input, not react to an agenda prepared by others. "When they are being force fed," says Keyworth, they have to say "that's not what we want."

When audit committees are dealing with their controllers or CFOs, they have to insist upon being given the correct information and, he says, "take advantage of those private sessions that they have with, for instance, the internal auditor and, most certainly, with the external auditors." Meetings should focus on risks and issues, with committee members requesting and reading specified information circulated and discussed in advance, rather than relying on management and auditor presentations. Private meetings are also encouraged to facilitate open and candid communication among committee members.

While audit committees avoid taking on the tasks of management, most need to sharply step up their oversight involvement in order to have the appropriate level of knowledge and interaction implicit in the concept and to comply properly with Sarbanes-Oxley.

AUDIT COMMITTEE ORGANIZATION AND OPERATION

The organization and operation of an audit committee is at the top of our pyramid framework in the diagram we presented earlier. In considering these elements, the board will necessarily want to ensure that the audit committee is comprised of the right individuals, and be satisfied that they are experienced, ethical, inquisitive and independent. New U.S. stock exchange, SEC, and Sarbanes-Oxley requirements take this even further. The U.S. stock exchange listing standards state that audit committees must have at least three independent, financially literate directors, one of whom must have "financial expertise."

Such requirements lead to more questions. What, for example, does it mean to be independent?

Under Sarbanes-Oxley, an audit committee member may not accept, directly or indirectly, any "consulting, advisory, or other compensatory fee" from either the company or any of its subsidiaries beyond the fee he or she receives from serving on the board, the committee itself, or any other board committee. In addition, Sarbanes-Oxley states that audit committee members can have no other affiliation with the company or its subsidiaries outside of his or her board role. Heaping the pile further, each of the three major U.S. exchanges—the New York Stock Exchange (NYSE), National Association of Securities Dealers (Nasdaq), and American Stock Exchange (AMEX)—have all proposed additional independence rules applicable to listed companies.

Two of the NYSE proposals require that:

☐ Employees have a five-year waiting period before being considered independent.

☐ Service on more than three public audit committees requires disclosure in proxy.

But while there appear to be no shortage of provisions concerning independence, a number of gray areas remain. For example, let's say Bob is on the audit committee of a multinational corporation that we'll call "Shopper's World," which has many broadly diversified consumer businesses. Bob has been a committed and active member of the Shopper's World audit committee for a few years now, but his "day job" is serving as CFO for another broadly diversified company, Universal Finance. This other company has a small overseas division that Shopper's World has just engaged to consult with its Israeli division on financing a regional product line.

Has Bob's independence on the Shopper's World board been compromised by the "indirect compensation" to his company's division? What if Bob's niece Jean, who graduated magna cum laude from Tuck and landed a job with Bain, ended up as a lower-level associate on the Bain engagement with Shopper's World. Would that violate Bob's independence?

There's no straight up or down answer to questions like these without involving skilled and experienced advisers. Make sure that you seek counsel when such questions arise, as they inevitably will.

In addition to independence considerations, Sarbanes-Oxley and the SEC's rules also impose the disclosure requirement that at least one committee member be an "audit committee financial expert." In their reporting, the company must state:

☐ Whether at least one member of the audit committee is an "audit committee financial expert."

☐ That person's name.

☐ If the company doesn't have one, an explanation why.

☐ Whether the "audit committee financial expert" is independent.

At present there are no penalties for not having an audit committee financial expert, but most companies prefer not to bare themselves publicly. This leaves some board members wondering whether they have an audit committee financial expert on hand and how they might go about spotting one if they did. Sarbanes-Oxley provides some guidance and identifies the board of directors as the party responsible for deciding whether its audit committee has at least one member who fits the criteria of an audit committee financial expert. The SEC's rules implementing Section 407 of Sarbanes-Oxley states that to be considered a financial expert one must have all of these five attributes:

1. Understand Generally Accepted Accounting Principles (GAAP) and financial statements

2. Be able to assess the application of GAAP in connection with the accounting for estimates, accruals, and reserves

3. Have experience preparing, auditing, analyzing, or evaluating financial statements with generally comparable breadth and complexity of accounting issues expected to be raised by the issuer's financial statements, or have experience actively supervising those engaged in such activities

4. Understand internal control over financial reporting

5. Understand audit committee functions

Robert Mittelstaedt is a vice dean and director of Wharton's Executive Education program and has helped run several governance programs. But even he notes that while "I'm reasonably knowledgeable, I'm not going to be able to qualify under the Sarbanes-Oxley definition of 'financial expert.' And most accounting professors wouldn't qualify either because the regulations define a financial expert as someone who has been an auditor or a CFO or CEO of a public company of similar size and has had responsibility for signing off on financial statements. I'm sure there are a lot of boards looking hard at their audit committee members to see who will meet those qualifications."[2] If you are on the audit committee of a public company and have questions about how to comply with this provision, be sure that you're getting the help and advice you need.

Audit Committee Assessment

Most charters include an annual evaluation. This allows committees to review their membership, their relationship with management and with their internal and external auditors, and, in light of recent regulations, their mandated whistleblower procedures. Formal assessments should include an audit committee self-assessment, as well as assessments by the board, the CFO, the CEO, and both internal and external auditors.

Cultivating a Climate of Constructive Dissent

In the previous chapter, we discussed the importance of setting the "tone at the top." There, we were talking about corporate culture and instilling the right ethical and risk management mind-set. Let us be more explicit here with regard to audit committees. We feel it imperative to create what some have called "a culture of dissent." In many well-meaning companies there is often no definable risk structure, but rather, a pattern of tacit communications between the audit committee and management and the audit committee and its internal/external auditors. "Setting the tone" in this case means establishing forthrightly the committee's objectivity and independence, its expectations from the various parties it oversees and those that support it, and its objectives.

Pattie Dunn, HP board member and vice chairman of Barclays Global Investors, uses the expression "slightly adversarial" to describe the committee oversight role. She understands that many audit committee members complain that management pushes back at them and they're struggling to gain the right traction. But she feels that directors simply have to come to expect this. There will be resistance on the part of management. It's not that management is bad or uncooperative. It's just human nature. Jay Keyworth feels the same way: "It's natural. Board members are inherently people who spend only part of their time overseeing the company. Inside, however, people are spending 100 percent of their time managing the business." It's a mismatch, he feels, but a healthy one.

Cultivating a culture of dissent can be the hardest step, because it can get in the way of otherwise collegial relations, and a committee member might feel awkward questioning management on topics he or she hadn't questioned in the past. This is yet another reason why an established and clearly documented framework can be invaluable.

Blowing the Whistle

Then there's the matter of whistleblower communications. Surveys have shown that many audit committees have yet to address their whistleblower program. Nonetheless, the new regulations require that audit committees have a formal process in place before the date of their first annual shareholders meeting after January 15, 2004, but in any event no later than October 31, 2004. The rule is intended to enable employees and others to take their concerns directly to the audit committee with the knowledge that procedures are in place so that their complaints will be acted upon and they will be protected from retaliation. At a minimum, companies are required to:

1. Ensure there is a satisfactory process for the receipt, retention, and treatment of complaints received regarding accounting, internal accounting controls, or auditing matters regardless of source

2. Ensure there is a satisfactory process for the confidential and anonymous submission by employees of concerns regarding questionable accounting or auditing matters

Some companies appoint an ombudsperson—a senior person vested with the right authority—often in the form of in-house counsel or chief compliance or ethics officer, to represent the employee before the audit committee. Other companies use an outside service to help them develop and manage their whistleblower communications.

A well-conceived hotline may include some of the following features:

Policy. The board should sign off on where and to whom given reports/concerns are directed.

Toll-free service. An employee doesn't want to have to pay to air his or her concerns.

24/7 service. Employees may wish to make calls from home if they feel uncomfortable doing so from the workplace.

"Real-time" assistance. An immediate live response is often superior to leaving a message and having it passed on to compliance personnel, particularly in cases of clear-cut questions, such as those involving gifts.

Qualifications. The individuals answering calls should be professional and qualified to take such calls. Some systems use full-time employees with specific experience in the area. Others outsource the process to an independent service with expertise in managing and responding to these types of calls.

Emergency notification. The hotline should be able to alert an appropriate person of authority, such as General Counsel or Chief of Security, if a call is of an extremely serious nature.

Confidentiality/anonymity. Anonymous calls should be accepted. Callers should be giving a case tracking number that the caller can reference in subsequent follow-ups.

Publicity. The company should promote its hotline with communications such as hotline posters, wallet cards, through the corporate intranet, and so forth.

FINANCIAL REPORTING RISK ASSESSMENT

Following the organization and operation of an audit committee, this is the second rung on our pyramid framework for effective audit committee oversight.

Wendy Lane was on the audit committee of Tyco during the company's dramatic fall. She is also a former managing director of Donaldson Lufkin & Jenrette, the chairman of the investment firm Lane Holdings, and a director of Laboratory Corporation of America. In an interview with John Engen of *Corporate Board Member* magazine, Lane was asked if she would shy away from serving on other audit committees because of the perceived risks. She responded: "Some people are afraid of heights, but I've already fallen off the cliff, and I've seen that you hit bottom and survive. Maybe if you haven't been in a situation like Tyco, you're not as confident in your abilities. But if you're truly competent, you shouldn't be afraid."[3]

Lane, battle scarred from a committee that bore the impact of all manner of unanticipated risks, believes there is an absolute need for audit committee members to become more circumspect. She feels it's too easy for critics and others pointing their fingers at Tyco to assume the problems arose from a breakdown in controls and a lax audit committee asleep at the switch. In fact, a review of Tyco's audit committee shows they were pursuing many recommended best practices, but these alone proved not enough. And that's the lesson, Lane stresses. "Did our internal auditors report directly to the audit committee?" she was asked. "Yes," she replied. "Did we ask them tough questions?" Again, yes. "In fact," Lane goes on to say, "we asked them regularly, 'Is there anything we should know? Has there been any pressure put on you by management to do things you don't want to do? If these were your financial statements, would you do anything differently?' And the answer," she says, "was always 'No.'"

The problem was that the audit committee did not look broadly enough. As an audit committee member, it's easy to think you know about risk assessment and to assume that your company has the necessary controls in place. Look at Tyco, Lane adds. "Tyco was a $39 billion company that was geographically dispersed, decentralized, in lots of different industries and countries. Where do you think the risk will be? In the field, right? So that's what the audit program was focused on. But the risk wasn't in the field; it was at home." And it's some of these "nontraditional" areas that audit committee members need to include in their review.

As audit committee members consider management misconduct, they will need to reflect on some of the more commonly documented areas, including:

☐ Trading of company securities (e.g., insider trading, fraud)

☐ Conflicts of interest

☐ Travel and entertainment

☐ Related party transactions

☐ Personal use of company assets

As part of the financial reporting risk assessment process, audit committees should cast a wide net, one that reflects the undulations of their business and sector. They should then consider whether management's approach to gathering information on and treating those risks is adequate. They should also check to see if the company's risk management function, CRO, or internal audit department has vetted it. Finally, they should satisfy themselves that management has a means of pinpointing the most material risks and what their and management's role is in coordinating identified actions.

In keeping with the strategic risk management approach recommended in this book, committee members can build a formal process around their financial reporting risk-assessment tasks that classify the nature, significance (from insignificant to catastrophic), and likelihood (remote to almost certain) of risks. They can then rank the risks based on their immediacy and impact, and focus on what response (avoidance, acceptance, transference, mitigation), internal control, or processes have been put in place or need to be put in place to treat the risks. Committee members should also factor the cost benefit of action over inaction into the evaluation, as well as the impact of residual, untreated risks—such as the remaining risk after management actions, process, and controls have been considered.

The Matrix

Fortunately, while an audit committee's overall effectiveness comes from its ability to prioritize activities based on financial reporting risks, one doesn't need a supercomputer to manage the task. One approach recommended by the Audit Committee Institute is to use a simple matrix structure to list the most significant financial reporting risks facing the company and the audit committee oversight activities associated with those risks.

In practice, an audit committee begins the process by meeting with external and internal auditors as well as with financial management to identify the six or 10 most significant financial reporting risks facing the company, including risks related to fraudulent financial reporting. This set of risks then forms the backbone of the matrix. Against this top six or 10, the audit committee populates the matrix rows with the various risk treatment activities they plan over the year and fills in the columns with the dates of each planned audit committee meeting, as depicted below.

The row-column intersections capture the meeting at which each activity and risk will be addressed. This matrix is then cross-referenced to the audit committee's own charter to ensure that all the activities in the charter are addressed during the year. During each audit committee meeting, each of the top risks would be reassessed to review where the committee stands in overseeing the company's response.

In fashioning the matrix it's useful to have some questions to guide the process. Here are some basic ones to keep in mind:

The Matrix: A Template					
KEY RISKS	SEPT. MTG. ACTIONS	DEC. MTG. ACTIONS	MARCH MTG. ACTIONS	JUNE MTG. ACTIONS	ANNUAL MEETING RESOLVE/ UPDATE
Risk 1	Action				Mitigated
Risk 2		Action			Transferred
Risk 3			Action	Action	Avoided
Risk 4		Action			Mitigated
Risk 5				Action	Pending
Risk 6	Action		Action		Transferred

Source: KPMG LLP © 2003

1. What is our tolerance for financial reporting risks? Have we communicated our tolerance to operating and financial management and the internal and external auditors? Does everyone understand and agree? Is "tone at the top" consistent with our risk tolerance?

2. Does our culture encourage open and candid discussion of our financial reporting risks and processes, including expression of concerns by individuals at all levels in the organization?

3. Do we know what our financial reporting risks are?

4. Have we considered appropriately the incentive/pressures and opportunities for fraud in our company as well as the attitudes/rationalizations of management and employees related to fraud?

5. How does the audit committee define significant financial reporting risk?

6 Do we understand the interrelationships of our financial reporting risks to each other and to other risks facing the company?

7. Do we know who our risk owners are? Do we have controls in place to manage the risks? Do we have processes in place for measuring and monitoring risk?

8. What is the perspective of the person or department overseeing risk?

9. How do our incentive programs affect risk management?

10. Does our understanding of financial reporting risk permeate our organization and culture?

11. Does each individual understand his or her role and responsibility for managing financial reporting risk?

12. Is financial reporting risk a priority consideration whenever business processes are changed or improved?

INTERNAL CONTROL OVER FINANCIAL REPORTING

Internal control over financial reporting—the third rung of our pyramid framework on effective audit committee oversight—and the audit committee's oversight of this process is dramatically changing with the passage of Sarbanes-Oxley and its mandate for management and external auditor reporting on management's assessment of the company's internal control over financial reporting. As SEC Commissioner Paul Atkins said in a speech in March 2003: "Internal controls and the culture of an organization are basic structural aspects to reinforce the inherent nature of most people to do the right thing."[4]

Today, oversight of this process is facilitated because of better defined responsibility and accountability for internal control, and as a result of better management procedures that support annual "effectiveness reporting." Indeed, as a result of the SEC rules implementing Sarbanes-Oxley Section 404, the annual report filed with the SEC must contain:

☐ A statement from management that lays out management's responsibility for establishing and maintaining an adequate internal control over financial reporting.

☐ The framework (e.g., COSO—The Committee of Sponsoring Organizations of the Treadway Commission's report, *Internal Control—Integrated Framework*) used by management to evaluate the effectiveness of internal control over financial reporting.

☐ Management's assessment, as of year-end, of the effectiveness of the internal control over financial reporting.

The company's independent auditors must then attest to and report on management's assessment in accordance with standards established by the Public Company Accounting Oversight Board (PCAOB).

Thus, before the independent auditor can complete a report on management's assessment of internal control over financial reporting in accordance with recommendations for revised auditing standards provided by the AICPA Auditing Standards Board to the PCAOB, management must meet certain conditions for engagement performance. These conditions require that management accept responsibility for the effectiveness of internal control over financial reporting, evaluate internal control effectiveness using suitable criteria, support its evaluation with sufficient evidence, and present a written assertion about the effectiveness of its internal control over financial reporting.

We will go into greater detail on internal control over financial reporting in Chapter 9. For now, it should be noted that in executing their oversight role as it concerns Sarbanes-Oxley Section 404, the audit committee might want to ask management the following questions to ensure that it has thoroughly thought through their compliance:

1. How detailed was the company's planning for the internal control documentation and evaluation process?

2. Has the company dedicated sufficient resources to adequately document and evaluate internal control in sufficient detail?

3. What is the planned involvement of the internal auditor in the internal control documentation and evaluation effort? Do they have appropriate training and resources to be effective in that role?

4. What type of in-house training will be provided at the operational level to help ensure that employees performing internal control-related tasks understand the importance and impact of their function?

5. Who within senior management is accountable for the internal control project?

6. Describe the significant controls associated with the significant risks considered in the risk assessment process.

7. Have any significant internal control deficiencies or material weaknesses been identified? Have they been corrected? Have any not been corrected, and if so, why not? Does the external auditor agree?

8. How detailed is the external auditor's planning for the audit of internal control?

9. Have management and the external auditor coordinated their plans?

10. Based on where we are today, does it appear that management and the external auditors will be able to meet the internal control reporting deadlines?

As Richard Bressler, CFO of Viacom, concludes: "It is critical that you conduct your business in a way that ensures credibility, that the books of record support the numbers that you report, that you have no issues with foreign corrupt practices, that you have sound internal control systems, and that every transaction gets recorded the way it's supposed to be recorded."

AUDIT PROCESS OVERSIGHT

In this section we'll discuss the bottom rung of our pyramid framework on effective audit committee oversight.

Benjamin Franklin said: "One of life's great tragedies is the murder of a beautiful theory by a gang of brutal facts." As the audit committee works with and reviews the results of both its internal and external auditors, they are tasked with satisfying themselves that indeed the facts of the case hold. To execute their charge, the audit committee must be empowered with the right authority—not only implicitly, but also explicitly. Implicitly, a direct reporting relationship must exist between internal audit and the audit committee, one that allows sufficient opportunity for the committee to approve the annual internal audit work plan and ensure that its scope and budget is adequate to address the financial reporting risks facing the company. Explicitly, we believe fundamentally that the committee should have veto power over the hiring and firing of the company's chief audit executive.

Moreover, audit committees are directly responsible to hire, pay, and, if necessary, dismiss the external auditor. Without these empowerments, the audit committee's enforcement powers will lack the needed weight.

The external audit relationship must also be managed with a view toward assessing the accounting firm's independence, ability, experience, and responsiveness. The SEC, in rules implementing Section 301 of Sarbanes-Oxley, adopted requirements that (1) the audit committee of a listed issuer will need to be directly responsible for the appointment, compensation, retention, and oversight of the external auditor; and (2) the external auditor reports directly to the audit committee.

The audit committee's approach to its oversight responsibilities, and determination of the extent of desired involvement, are left to the discretion of the audit committee. Oversight responsibilities include resolution of disagreements between management and the auditor regarding financial reporting and the authority to retain the auditor, which includes the power not to retain (or to terminate) the auditor. In addition, in connection with these oversight responsibilities, the audit committee must have ultimate authority to approve all audit engagement fees and terms.

With the new regulations, audit committees are also tasked with approving any nonaudit activities performed by the external auditor. The external auditor now has a responsibility to go to the audit committee for preapproval of all such services.

CONCLUSION

Effective oversight recognizes that financial reporting is the culmination of a process, the components of which can be summarized as follows:

☐ Financial reporting risk-assessment process

☐ Accounting systems to capture information

☐ System of internal control, including "tone at the top"

☐ Evaluation and interpretation of data

☐ External and internal reporting of financial data

Thinking about it visually, the participants in this process can be viewed as the "legs" of a stool comprising responsible disclosure and oversight. The three legs are: (1) management, including internal audit; (2) the independent external auditor; and (3) the audit committee. Recognizing, maintaining, and coordinating the unique roles of each "leg" are critical to the integrity of the process.

Management, supported by internal audit, is charged with implementing, maintaining, and monitoring the financial reporting process. Under this umbrella comes responsibility for the company's internal control structure and financial reporting risk management policies. Then management, often supported by the internal auditor, is tasked with attesting to the adequacy and effectiveness of those controls. The external auditor, accountable to the audit committee, audits and reports on the financial statements and management's assertion on internal control over financial reporting. The audit committee, accountable to the board and the shareholders, is left with oversight of all of the preceding. To fulfill its watchdog role, the audit committee must necessarily be free to coordinate with the internal and external audit in a way that allows it to retain the advantage of independent and objective oversight.

The Three Legs of Financial Reporting

AUDIT COMMITTEE
Provide oversight, challenge, and influence
"Tone at the top"
Financial reporting risk management
Adequacy of control environment
Adequacy of financial reporting process
Accounting policies and estimates
Unusual transactions
Financial management
Internal auditors
External auditors
Encourage continual improvement

(continued on next page)

The Three Legs of Financial Reporting *(continued)*

EXTERNAL AUDITOR

Audit of financial statements and related attestation on management's assertions on internal control over financial reporting in accordance with GAAS

Render opinion on financial statements

Attestation related to internal control over financial reporting

Audit committee communications

Test and challenge:

  Financial reporting

  Internal control over financial reporting

Improvement suggestions

MANAGEMENT

"Tone at the top"

Infrastructure to support financial reporting process

Financial reporting and risks, including internal control over financial reporting

Design

Implement

Maintain

Communicate

Evaluate and report

Internal Auditor

Evaluate internal control

Test financial reporting

Risk management process

Improvement suggestions

Source: KPMG LLP, 2003

CHAPTER 9

Inside Section 404

"We are at a pivotal point in the reestablishment of faith in the business and financial communities."

—William Donaldson, SEC Chairman

"Honey. Kids. Take care of each other and don't forget to feed the dog. I'll be back in about six months once I've finished my internal control over financial reporting review."

While this is a stretch, it's hard to overestimate the impact of Sarbanes-Oxley. Indeed, some have compared the reach and significance of Sarbanes-Oxley to the Securities Act of 1933. Certainly, few pieces of legislation have attracted such a wide base of interest. We may not remember what else the U.S. Congress did or did not pass in 2002, but chances are most Americans have heard of Senators Sarbanes and Oxley and their eponymous act. Chances are also good that the finance and audit groups of most public companies are giving one section of Sarbanes-Oxley particular focus, namely, Section 404.

INSIDE SECTION 404

In June 2003 the SEC released its final rules governing management's report on internal control over financial reporting. The rules did three things:

☐ Implemented the requirements of Section 404 of Sarbanes-Oxley

☐ Amended the officer certifications required by Sections 302 and 906 of Sarbanes-Oxley

☐ Delayed the originally proposed effective date for filing management's report on internal control over financial reporting

The last point, much anticipated, was responsible for a giant sigh of relief from the vast majority of issuers scrambling to effectively document, test, and evaluate their internal control over financial reporting.

The effect has been that companies, even those slow to begin the compliance exercise, are now opening their file drawers and embarking seriously on the process. This is all to the good, because even with extended deadlines, complying with Section 404 is a months-long exercise. Accelerated filers, generally companies with a "public float"[1] over $75 million, have to comply with the new rules for their fiscal years ending on or after June 15, 2004; December 31, 2004, for calendar year companies. All other issuers, including small-business and, foreign-private issuers, will be required to comply with the new rules for their fiscal years ending on or after April 15, 2005.

As companies are rapidly learning, preparing for an audit of internal control over financial reporting for the first time is a complex, resource-intensive, and time-consuming process. A prompt start is important if companies intend to complete a proper evaluation of internal control over financial reporting and allow time for their external auditors to complete their own work.

As Mark Hurd, CEO of NCR, states: "It's one thing to say that the financial information is correct and accurate to the best of my knowledge. It's another thing when I certify that the processes underneath it are fair and accurate. We have 130 legal constituencies where we do business and 21,000 separate accounts that financial information moves through. That is a lot of consolidation and reconciliation." He notes: "We're going through a lot of change right now to determine how we can audit that, and how we can put controls around that, so that we can sign it with assurance."

Alan L. Beller, director of the SEC's Division of Corporate Finance, underscored the nature of the challenge when speaking at a conference to corporate lawyers shortly after the final rules were announced. He said: "You and your company should have already started to devote attention and resources to implementation of the commission's most recent rules . . . Based on what we've seen and heard, companies will need the extra time even if they've already started."[2]

Under the final rules implementing Section 404, in each annual report filed with the SEC, management's report on internal control over financial reporting, public companies—

other than registered investment companies and asset-backed issuers—will have to include:

☐ A statement of management's responsibility for establishing and maintaining adequate internal control over financial reporting for the issuer.

☐ A statement identifying the framework, such as COSO (Committee of Sponsoring Organizations of the Treadway Commission's report, "Internal Control—Integrated Framework"), used by management to evaluate the effectiveness of internal control over financial reporting.

☐ Management's assessment of the effectiveness of internal control over financial reporting as of the end of the issuer's most recent fiscal year, which includes a statement as to whether or not the issuer's internal control over financial reporting is effective. This discussion must include disclosure of any material weakness in the issuer's internal control over financial reporting identified by management. Management is not permitted to conclude that the issuer's internal control over financial reporting is effective if there are one or more material weaknesses in the issuer's internal control over financial reporting.

☐ A statement that the issuer's independent auditor has issued an attestation report on management's assessment of internal control over financial reporting.

At heart we are talking about the quality, accuracy, and transparency of financial information. And while one might agree with Oscar Wilde's wry comment that, "It is a very sad thing that nowadays there is so little useless information," evidence shows that companies are giving due attention to their information responsibilities.

In getting started, companies must first determine which methodology and framework to use for their internal control over financial reporting assessment. It is a matter over which the SEC was deliberately quiet. Their intent was to make companies work through a program that best fit their situation rather than providing detailed requirements.

Nevertheless, the SEC does prevent one from wandering too far astray in this regard. Its rules lay out certain clear expectations in conducting an evaluation and developing an assessment requiring the company to "maintain evidential matter, including documentation, to provide reasonable support for management's assessment of the effectiveness of the registrant's internal control over financial reporting." Translated, this means that the onus is on management to provide clear and thorough documentation of both the design of internal control over financial reporting and the procedures and evaluation management has conducted to gauge their operating effectiveness.

While management also has discretion in choosing the control framework upon which to base its evaluation, the rules require that it be a suitable and recognized control framework established and developed by a body that has followed "due process procedures, including the broad distribution of the framework for public comment."[3] For the vast majority of companies, this means COSO, far and away the most commonly used framework in the United States today.

BRASS TACKS

Turning to the task of compliance, the following six-stage approach may be considered by management, keeping in mind the obvious point that companies must take into account their own business and operating conditions. Likewise, for a host of reasons, management should be sure to consult with its legal, accounting, and other advisers before embarking on a specific methodology and before concluding on any matters involving interpretation of the provisions of Sarbanes-Oxley. Ultimately, it is management's responsibility to design a process sufficient to meet its needs.

Six Stages to Addressing Section 404[4]

1. Plan and scope the evaluation.
2. Document your controls.
3. Evaluate the design and operating effectiveness of your controls.
4. Identify and correct deficiencies.
5. Prepare management's report on internal control over financial reporting.
6. Prepare for the independent auditor's report on management's assessment of internal control over financial reporting.

Planning and Scoping the Evaluation

The first and arguably most important task begins with appointing an owner to run the evaluation. Our experience has shown that the most successful implementations occur when management elects a senior executive as the overall project owner. Ideally, this person is someone of authority, with access to the top of the organization and with an ear to the company's strategy and objectives. Tactically, this ensures that the process becomes a priority initiative at the staff level and that actions are taken with the right alacrity.

Underneath this figure, management should consider appointing a project manager and pulling together a select group of cross-functional resources from departments such as operations, finance, human resources, information systems, tax, legal, and internal audit. These individuals comprise the core, dedicated team. All should possess a good understanding of controls evaluation and the evaluation framework, such as COSO. Where this understanding is lacking, training should be supplied to augment it.

TIP

Be sure to factor in key tax processes and controls in conducting your planning exercise since tax generally represents one of the largest expenses on a company's financial statements—the impact often extends beyond corporate income taxes and provisions to sales or value-added taxes, and beyond.

Once established, this group's next assignment is laying out the rules of engagement for the rest of the exercise or, more specifically, the policies and procedures for its evaluation and internal communication process. Only after this basic infrastructure is in place can the group turn to its next major task, that of identifying the company's significant controls and business units, locations, and geographies to be included within the evaluation's scope. It is important that the plan allow sufficient time for management to complete its evaluation and take corrective action, and for the external auditor to complete its work.

As you go through this stage, maintain contact with your auditors. It is far better to make any needed course corrections here than later on, when waist-deep in the process.

In sum:

1. Establish project governance and put in place an ongoing project management approach.

2. Select an internal control framework to provide suitable control criteria for evaluation.

3. Assemble a cross-disciplinary team, trained in the internal control framework to be used in the evaluation, and led by a senior, active, management figure.

4. Determine the plan, policies, and scope of your approach.

5. Run the plan, policies, and scope past your external auditor before proceeding.

Document How Controls Have Been Assessed

Documentation of your company's internal control over financial reporting is an essential element of management's evaluation process. It provides evidence that controls related to management's assertion, including changes to those controls, have been identified and can be monitored by the company. Inadequate documentation may result in a significant deficiency or material weakness in internal control.

The documentation stage is likely to consume a significant amount of your team's time. Internal control documentation should address all significant controls that are designed to prevent or detect misstatement or fraud in significant financial statement account balances, classes of transactions, and disclosures. For companies utilizing the COSO control framework, documentation should include all relevant financial statement assertions and each of the five COSO internal control components: control environment, risk assessment, control activities, information and communications, and monitoring. The documentation should encompass the design of the control, including the control objective, risks addressed, responsible parties, the related segregation of duties, and the initiating, processing, and recording of significant account balances and classes of transactions.

TIP

Since this can be a formidable task, many companies opt to automate their approach. A variety of suitable software exists to gather, organize and report data in a consistent format, tailored to COSO and Section 404 requirements.

Where possible, establish a single, companywide documentation standard for capturing and reporting information. Management can also enlist the help of their external auditor in assisting with gathering information and preparing documentation. But management must be actively involved in and assume responsibility for the entire process, both to satisfy independence requirements as well as to reinforce institutional learning.

In sum:

1. Consider establishing one uniform standard across the enterprise.

2. Consider using an automated tool for efficiency.

3. Ensure that the documentation exercise covers entitywide controls—controls in place to monitor operations and to oversee the control environment and risk assessment at the locations or business units—and design of significant controls related to management's assertions regarding internal control over financial reporting, including:
   a. Each of the components of internal control
   b. How significant transactions are initiated, recorded, processed, and reported
   c. The controls designed to prevent or detect errors or fraud in significant account balances, classes of transactions, and disclosures
   d. Controls, including general controls, on which other significant controls are dependent
   e. The financial statement closing process
   f. Safeguarding controls

Evaluate the Design and Operating Effectiveness of Controls

Management will need to evaluate the design and operating effectiveness of internal control over financial reporting, including completeness of the control documentation. It will also need to document results of the evaluation. Design effectiveness refers to whether a control is suitably designed to prevent or detect material misstatements. Operating effectiveness is concerned with how the control was applied, the consistency with which it was applied, and by whom it was applied; essentially, whether the control is functioning as designed. While the rules do not specify a methodology for evaluating operating effectiveness, inquiry alone will not be sufficient.

TIP

The COSO framework provides helpful evaluation criteria and examples for the five main internal control components —control environment, risk assessment, control activities, information and communication, and monitoring.

Where companies might have been hoping for flexibility in rotating evaluations on an annual basis, the external auditor will expect management's evaluation to encompass each one of the significant business locations and business units and all significant controls in connection with each assertion about effectiveness of internal control over financial reporting.

In addition, management is also prohibited from using the results from its own independent auditor's control tests as the basis for its conclusion on design or operating effectiveness.

In sum:

1. Evaluate design effectiveness of internal control over financial reporting.

2. Evaluate operation of controls based on procedures sufficient to verify their operating effectiveness. All significant locations and all significant controls must be evaluated in connection with each assertion about the effectiveness of internal control. Inquiry alone will not constitute an adequate evaluation.

3. Document the results of the evaluation.

Identify and Correct Deficiencies

As with the prior documentation stage, automation can be your best friend at this juncture, particularly if you have taken the initiative to establish documentation, control, and reporting standards across your enterprise. An internal control deficiency may be either a design or operating deficiency. Management should establish a process by which deficiencies are identified and accumulated across the entire company, including all locations and business units evaluated. Management should evaluate the significance of these identified deficiencies, considered together, on the design and operating effectiveness of internal control. In addition, management also should determine whether financial statement misstatements have occurred as a result of the identified control deficiencies.

The factors in deciding whether an internal control deficiency is a significant deficiency or a material weakness requires both a detailed understanding of the relevant facts and circumstances and a considerable amount of judgment on the part of management. To demonstrate sufficient evidence for its conclusion, management should document the reason that a particular control deficiency (or an aggregation of internal controls with a common feature or attribute) was not corrected or did not preclude management from concluding that internal control over financial reporting is operating effectively. Management should also discuss with the company's audit committee the process for identifying and correcting deficiencies.

TIP

Be sure to test any remedies in "live" setting before concluding on then.

When management takes corrective action to remedy a control deficiency, the corrected control should be in place and operating for a sufficient period of time prior to the assertion date for management to evaluate the corrected control and conclude that the control is operating effectively as of the assertion date.

Management should remember that internal control, no matter how well designed and operated, can provide only reasonable assurance to management and the board of directors regarding achievement of a company's control objectives.

The likelihood of achievement is affected by limitations inherent to internal control. These limitations include the fact that human judgment in decision making can be faulty, and that breakdowns in internal control can occur because of human error. Additionally, controls can be circumvented by the collusion of two or more people or by management override of internal control.

In sum:

1. Identify control deficiencies.

2. Determine which control deficiencies are of such a magnitude, quantitatively or qualitatively or both, that they constitute significant deficiencies or material weaknesses, including:

   a. Carry out a process by which deficiencies are identified and accumulated across the entire organization, including all locations and business units evaluated

   b. Aggregate deficiencies with common attributes or features

   c. Evaluate (using both quantitative and qualitative factors) the significance of those identified deficiencies (considered together) on the operating effectiveness of internal control

   d. Determine whether financial statement misstatements have occurred as a result of the identified internal control deficiencies

   e. Communicate findings to the audit committee, independent auditor, and others, if applicable

Management Report on Internal Control over Financial Reporting

This is the pinnacle of the paper trail, the point at which management sets forth in writing its responsibility for maintaining a sound system of internal control and confidence over that system's effectiveness.

Once management has completed its evaluation, it should consider the reporting requirements of Section 404. The final rule on Section 404 requires that each annual report filed with the SEC contain an internal control report that contains the elements described earlier in this chapter. The SEC did not provide uniform language for management's report. Instead, each company's report should be particular to its own circumstances.

TIP

Financial institutions reporting under FDICIA should be aware that the reporting requirements on the effectiveness of internal control over financial reporting mandated by that Act differ in certain respects from those set forth in Section 404.

If management or the external auditor identifies a material weakness in internal control over financial reporting, management may need to consider the weakness in the context of its previous Section 302 certifications in consultation with legal counsel. Management should also consider the consequences of any identified weaknesses in light of the books and records and internal controls requirements of the Securities Exchange Act of 1934 and other laws.

Auditor's Report on Management's Assessment of Internal Control over Financial Reporting

The independent auditor will obtain an understanding of the process that management used in determining which controls were significant, how management evaluated and documented them, and will make a judgment as to whether management's conclusions were reasonable.

TIP

Do not underestimate the complexity or time involved in complying with Section 404. An early start is essential.

The auditor will then obtain an understanding of internal control over financial reporting, evaluate the design effectiveness of controls, and perform tests to validate that the stated controls are indeed operating effectively. The implications of any deficiencies will be assessed to see what bearing, if any, they have on the effectiveness of the company's internal control over financial reporting. The external auditor's report on management's assertion on internal control over financial reporting will be included in the annual report filed by the enterprise with the SEC. The audit of internal control over financial reporting is a significant undertaking.

With this stage completed, a company will have satisfied its Section 404 reporting requirement, and the hardworking audit and finance staff can return home weary but confident that they have carried out their duties.

IMPLEMENTING SECTION 404

For someone who has traveled a fair ways down the trail, we turn to Peter Oppenheimer, senior vice president of finance at Apple Computer.

When you talk to Oppenheimer, you hear the word "execution" a lot. As Apple's point man on Sarbanes-Oxley compliance, he was intent that the company's program commence long before the SEC's final rules on Section 404 came out. "For a little while," he says, "it looked like we would have had to do our certification this coming September, and we would have been ready. We took the project very, very seriously."

Oppenheimer points to a few factors that helped Apple through the complicated compliance process. Topping the list were attention at the top, discipline, and communication. He says that the company's "focused approach to managing this project at the most senior levels of finance management," combined with "an aggressive timetable," and "reporting regularly to our audit committee," were pivotal.

In terms of the aggressive timetable, Oppenheimer remarks: "After adopting the COSO framework, we focused our entire finance leadership team early in calendar 2003 on a project plan." Together, he says, he and his team "pulled out and refreshed every one of the company's finance and accounting policies." Over the course of "a good six months," the team reviewed and documented each of the company's existing controls and procedures.

It was an admittedly brisk pace. Helping them to stay on course, Oppenheimer stresses was "having senior finance management directing an internal team to review and document policies and procedures and controls." Without question, he emphasizes, engagement at the top is critical. The next most important step "is ensuring cross-functional integration of the controls to improve risk management."

In terms of day-to-day staffing, Apple didn't take people off line to run the process. Rather, they embedded the function within Oppenheimer's own staff. Through a two-hour staff meeting conducted weekly from January to May 2003, Oppenheimer himself stayed closely involved. He notes: "The first 30 to 45 minutes each week were spent going through where we were on the policy rewrite and where we were on the procedure rewrite, area by area." He adds: "The senior finance management team reviewed things weekly and just banged it out and did a good job."

Still, Oppenheimer and team were careful to keep key people regularly informed. "We spent a lot of time with our audit partner up front agreeing on what a procedure should look like," he says, "because the last thing we wanted was to have a structure of a procedure that he wasn't okay with." Oppenheimer also made a point of regularly briefing the audit committee on their progress in writing procedures and policies: "We had about 90 finance policies to review, and we updated the audit committee along the way. We also updated them on procedures around the world when those were done."

Oppenheimer kept internal audit closely involved as well: "All of the procedures were reviewed by internal audit. They were written by the line teams, reviewed by the internal audit, questions sent back, then finalized and issued."

With the finish line in view, Oppenheimer feels good about the company's progress, noting that external sources tell him "we're in the top tier of the Fortune 500 in terms of where we are on this."

Still, before retiring the abacus, most business leaders agree on the need to tote up the cost benefit of the compliance exercise and one's procedures in response to it.

COST BENEFIT

The cost of implementing Section 404 of Sarbanes-Oxley is a matter of debate. To some degree, it depends on the size of your organization. Large companies, particularly those with sizable finance staffs and a highly developed reporting system, may well be able to absorb the extra documentation and reporting requirements within their staffs and budget. Nonetheless, Margaret Johnsson, chairman and CEO of the Johnsson Group and former internal auditor at Beatrice Foods, estimates that the initial implementation expenses for a "typical" $3 billion company range from $1.1 to $3.5 million, including factors such as outside consulting, internal audit expansion, and changes in the scope and fees of the external audit.[5]

For smaller companies, however, the costs can extend beyond dollars. There are some who believe the relative weight of compliance is unduly burdensome for these companies, many of which lack the large staffs and discrete functional expertise of larger companies. As a result, compliance often falls on top executives. This can force them to lift their focus from strategy, marketing, and other competitive issues, potentially impairing their ability to keep pace with larger, better-resourced competitors who more easily "multitask."

Jeff Henley, CFO of Oracle, agrees. While Oracle's compliance program is extremely advanced, Henley feels smaller businesses have a tougher challenge. "The problem for small companies," he says, "is that Sarbanes is unbelievably heavy. They just don't have the infrastructure and the people and the talent to deal with all this regulation." Accordingly, Henley believes that "Sarbanes has placed a proportionately heavier burden on them."

Still, despite the costs, financial and otherwise, the rigor and discipline required from Sarbanes-Oxley is undoubtedly yielding significant benefits. There are many who have used the Sarbanes-Oxley requirements to streamline their processes, eliminate waste, establish single instance reporting, and enact other operations improvements. One such company slimmed down from 13 separate general ledger systems to one integrated global system. It was rewarded with huge cost savings in its sales and administrative function alone.

Other benefits are more subtle. These include cultural changes and the permeating of greater organizational risk sensitivity. Companies are building awareness of the major risk factors that could impact negatively on them, and spreading the notion that risk ownership is everyone's responsibility. Even nonfinance people are taking a much closer look at the disclosures in MD&As, along with the rest of the Form 10-Ks and Form10-Qs, and understanding how various risks impact their business.

CONCLUSION

Sarbanes-Oxley intends for all those involved in financial reporting to work together to foster accountability and meaningful transparency. Once the purview of accountants, internal control over financial reporting now involves many parts of the organization. Executed well, through meaningful and accurate reporting, better and more efficient operations, and a higher level of engagement and individual ownership throughout the business, the value extends to the whole system, with all parties—management, employees, and, most of all, shareholders—standing to benefit.

CHAPTER 10

Internal Control—
Insights
from the Field

*"When you do the common things in life in an
uncommon way, you will command the attention of the world."*

—George Washington Carver

"When we all got back to Apple about six years ago,"
Finance SVP Peter Oppenheimer says, "We made a
lot of improvements in the company, in areas such as real-
time information systems, very strong management processes,
policies and procedures, and a high degree of accountability.
From an operational perspective, these have succeeded in
lowering the volatility in our results and improving execution."

Although Apple's resurgence as a dominant tech player
predated Sarbanes-Oxley and the corporate scandals of recent
years, Oppenheimer's attitude and approach about internal

control was echoed by the other leading finance executives with whom we spoke. Even though today's tense environment may cause some companies to retrench, the best are forging ahead with rigorous and thoughtful reviews of their internal control, and in the process, are injecting a great deal of resourcefulness into the effort.

INTERNAL CONTROL OVER FINANCIAL REPORTING

Internal control can be fairly said to cover a variety of areas from operational to financial control. The SEC in its final rules concerning the implementation of Section 404 gave us this definition for internal control over financial reporting.[1]

A process designed by, or under the supervision of, the issuer's principal executive and principal financial officers, or persons performing similar functions, and effected by the issuer's board of directors, management and other personnel, to provide reasonable assurance regarding the reliability of financial reporting and the preparation of financial statements for external purposes in accordance with generally accepted accounting principles and includes those policies and procedures that:

1. Pertain to the maintenance of records that in reasonable detail accurately and fairly reflect the transactions and dispositions of the assets of the issuer.

2. Provide reasonable assurance that transactions are recorded as necessary to permit preparation of financial statements in accordance with generally accepted accounting principles, and that receipts and expenditures of the issuer are being made only in accordance with authorizations of management and directors of the issuer.

3. Provide reasonable assurance regarding prevention or timely detection of unauthorized acquisition, use, or disposition of the issuer's assets that could have a material effect on the financial statements.

In formulating an effective internal control process, finance leaders rely on discipline, discernment, and diligence. From our research and observations, we note that internal control standards and procedures are increasingly being drawn from a company's formal risk assessment. We are witnessing finance departments revisiting the design, documentation, and evaluation of their controls—even beyond that stipulated by statutory requirements. We are observing the scope of control being expanded to include enhanced procedures for fraud prevention, deterrence, and detection. And we are seeing unquestioned recognition that, above all, management of internal control requires accountability. There must be an owner for each critical process or control, and that structure must be clearly communicated.

Placing the foregoing chapter on Section 404 into broader perspective, here are a range of thoughts, stories, and personal experiences "for leaders by leaders" on the subject of internal control and risk management.

Volatility in Perspective

Lessons from Apple Computer

Internal control exists in large part to help companies minimize unwanted shocks to the system. Yet, even in the notoriously volatile tech industry, risks can be mitigated and stability wrought by observing four steps, says Peter Oppenheimer of Apple.

The first of these steps, he notes, "is real-time information systems, controlling key operational areas, particularly in the supply chain, manufacturing, distribution, and sales functions, all of which can help to minimize financial risk." The second thing, he adds, is "a strong cross-functionally integrated management and control process around key points of failure and high risk areas, such as product development and planning." Next, he notes, is a need for "clearly defined operating and financial policies." And fourth and last, he stresses, a company must have a "culture of high integrity and accountability."

These sensible thoughts can help to anchor a company's thinking and approach on a macro level.

Controls in the Microcosm

For a glimpse inside the microcosm of internal control, we can think of few better examples than that of the complex post-merger integration of Compaq and Hewlett-Packard.

Lessons from the HP–Compaq Postmerger Integration Process

Even in this era of increased scrutiny on internal control, one is hard pressed to find a more high-risk or publicly scrutinized controls exercise than the postmerger integration between Hewlett-Packard and Compaq. It was a job designed to test even those of the stoutest constitutions. But then you meet former Compaq CFO Jeff Clarke, who, along with Webb McKinney, then head of HP's sales force, was chosen lead the integration program, and you begin to understand why things went so smoothly. As current EVP of Global Operations at HP, Clarke is a highly focused thinker who recognized early that making the integration work meant getting the details right.

Looking back on the process, he calls the postmerger planning program "an example of absolute discipline and rigor in an extremely tightly controlled process." Expounding, Clarke notes: "We established the most thoroughly planned merger in history and probably the tightest managed from a control process perspective. We created a structure of delegation and approval throughout our integration and we tracked it with absolute rigor and vigilance."

Far from occupying the bully pulpit, he and McKinney reported to a steering committee consisting of the former CEO of Compaq, Carly Fiorina; the CEO and chairman of HP; the CFO of the new firm; the head of HR of the new firm; and the CIO of the new firm. The team, says Clarke, "met once a week for a half day and drove all of the ratification decisions and saw the risks inherent and managed those risks." He adds: "We didn't take the risk of the merger lightly."

Whether it was working with his business unit, functional or international teams—the merger had 25 in all—Clarke notes that "probably the biggest thing was that every decision process and every part of the integration plan of record was tracked using a red, green, and yellow qualitative criteria with lots of quantitative results supporting it." A believer that the devil lay firmly in the details, Clarke made a point of ensuring that "every decision, such as phasing out Product A from HP and going with Product B from Compaq or adopting the general ledger process of HP or the general ledger process of Compaq, was brought in by its group, measured in a red, green, and yellow process flow, and then cascaded up the company."

In practice, Clarke continues, this meant that "on Mondays, the integration program team would review with each of the 25 teams how their programs were going and assessed the self grades those teams gave on red, green, and yellow." The leaders then made judgments as to their validity. "This second set of eyes," Clarke adds, "was used to assess whether we were being too hard on ourselves, giving too many reds or yellows and not enough greens, or being too light on ourselves on those programs with great control risks."

Following that review, the remaining important "red and yellow issues" were elevated to Clarke and McKinney's all-day Wednesday meeting, where items and progress were hashed out further before eventually flowing over to the steering committee.

Clarke indicates by way of example: "When an item was off track, such as a product transition, a vendor renegotiation, an IT system implementation, or a decision on Process A versus Process B, and that item came in at yellow or red, the issue cascaded first to the program team, second to Webb and myself, and third all the way to the Steering Committee when material." This helped the team's leaders retain an ongoing sense of where the issues were and, as Clarke puts it, "where they fell from an implementation risk standpoint and from a complexity standpoint."

Such a tight process and regular monitoring also allowed Clarke and company to map critical risk interdependencies. He says: "By mapping them, you could then see that a risk in Area A had a certain implication on Area B, and that while B was in green status, the interdependency with A would elevate that formerly benign risk to a yellow or red status." It might sound basic, but as Clarke emphasizes: "The interdependency was visible, so the rigor of that process, the almost PERT-chart-like interdependency mapping, and the tool of red, green, and yellow highlighting across each process, and each implementation step, really helped us manage the risks inherent in a very risky process."

While Clarke's internal control process was dedicated to managing the intricate details of a giant corporate merger, his experience has relevance for finance executives working through their own control review. Indeed, for all of us who regularly hear and endorse themes emphasizing the importance of a clear approach, leadership from the top, frequent monitoring, and rigorous execution, there's nothing like seeing these virtues applied to a highly charged, real-world setting to bring home the point.

On Systems, Standards, and
Interactive Control Risk Management

Lessons from Microsoft and Oracle

Microsoft also uses a weighting mechanism to review its internal control. In doing so, the tech giant brings its considerable information technology expertise to bear through a specially developed SharePoint site called IssueManager. "As internal audit goes through the various operations," controller Scott Di Valerio explains, "they come up with recommendations. These recommendations are put into our IssueManager site, each with a high, medium, or low rating, depending on their level of importance." They use the technology in part for efficiency and in part for risk protection. Indeed, with Microsoft's deep international presence, Di Valerio understands how important it is to keep documentation consistent across each of the company's global regions.

The weightings given in IssueManager are set through a collaboration process between the corporate controller and internal audit organizations. In addition, Di Valerio adds, "each recommendation is given an owner, a project manager, and a timeline" to resolve the issue. This allows all pertinent parties to go in and check status and sort the site by highs, mediums, lows—by the person who's responsible, by the date, and by which ones are resolved and closed off."

The results are then presented to Microsoft's audit committee. Says Di Valerio: "We share which issues are still open, which have been closed, and which need the most immediate attention." In addition, Di Valerio adds, the company uses the site to capture recommendations from its independent auditor arising from the audit, each of which is given the same weighting criteria. That way, he concludes, "we have a dynamic, up-to-date total each quarter." He can then follow up with issue owners by e-mail to get necessary items closed down.

Such interactive technology offers an improvement over the past, he says, where "people received both the independent auditor and internal auditor reports in static form—paper or e-mail—that was not easily followed up on. As a result, a lot of them would get filed until the next reporting cycle and then revisited. This way," he stresses, "the reports are not forgotten about. They're managed across the worldwide organization."

Not surprisingly, Oracle CFO Jeff Henley is another keen proponent of the use of technology in facilitating tighter internal control management. "The Treadway Commission," he says, "articulated the need for companies to have accurate, transparent financial statements." This puts finance executives in an age old bind: how to achieve both good internal controls while also achieving good cost effectiveness. It's a balance that Henley notes "can be a tall order to achieve."

Yet, as you'd expect from a leader in database management software, Henley asserts: "It's our contention that the best way to achieve the desired result is through a highly centralized set of systems and processes.

"Our belief," he says, "is that you need to simplify your systems and ideally have only one set of global applications using a single database." For most companies, of course, this is the Holy Grail, and many would concede Henley's point that "you can't get really good, rich information on your company if you've got a whole bunch of different systems all over the place, different general ledgers in different divisions, and different processes."

Part of the problem, in Henley's view, is a direct result of the technology buying surge in the '90s. "People spent a ton of money on technology," he says. "They bought new SAP or

PeopleSoft or Oracle, and what they're finding is after spending all that money they still don't have integrated systems. They don't have one global system." Instead, Henley says, "people are realizing that the scalability of the Web is not a technical challenge anymore. It was for a long time. Now it's just the challenge of getting all the business processes common, all the data common, and putting this all in one integrated system."

Oracle is busy practicing what it preaches. "We have some unique experience," Henley adds, "certainly as a software company, but more importantly having just actually gone through this process. We're now down to almost a single worldwide system—Japan comes in the fall," he notes. "So, we've got 60-some odd countries on a single set of financials, project accounting, HR, procurement, distribution, all in a global system run in a U.S. data center."

But Henley doesn't gloss over the difficulties: "It's been incredibly difficult." His staff has "aged enormously," he says, chuckling. "But we're getting close to seeing the real benefits both in terms of IT cost savings as well as in getting really good information out. You get there slowly but surely," he admits, "but you get a much tighter set of global processes.

"The point," he says, "is you can go and spend a lot of money documenting your processes and making sure that your internal controls are good, but we would argue that most companies are still too fragmented, divisionally and geographically, to get real efficiency and to get real transparency of rich information in a systematic way." From a control standpoint, Henley believes such disparate systems add to a company's volatility: "If you have 10 different systems and ten different processes versus one, it's just harder to get your arms around it, and the chance of things going wrong somewhere go up. You'll never be as vigilant with 10 different systems as you will with one. It's unaffordable.

"If you centralize your data," he continues, "you can put more resources in one place to make sure that you have adequate control. You can put more professionalism in the shared center. You can put more pressure on the local country managers to keep them from leaning on the finance directors to deviate, saying, 'I don't care what the process is, just do this.' They can't with one system. So all this centralization does help to mitigate risk."

As these comments together indicate, controlling the control system, as it were, driving consistency internally and across one's enterprise, ensuring a uniform issue capture-and-reporting format, all serve as an important lever in mitigating some of the natural volatility resident within an organization.

On Taking Ownership

Lessons from Sprint

Bob Dellinger, the CFO at Sprint, sees many best practices emerging in the way companies are responding to Sarbanes-Oxley: "Clearly, one major improvement is involving more people in reviewing our financial disclosures. We hold a number of reviews each quarter in connection with certification of our Form 10-Q or Form 10-K. We hold these reviews with business leaders, unit CFOs, and key functional leaders, to review and discuss our financial disclosures to ensure that they are complete, accurate, and transparent.

"These detailed discussions are involving more people in the review of our financial disclosures. It is a very healthy exercise, and our challenge going forward is to keep the certification process fresh." Dellinger makes a point of adding that the process works only if people are engaged. "Like all processes," he says, "you do it every quarter, and it can become stale. So, you've got to keep changing the process to reenergize it. You've got to shake it up a little."

Increasingly, there's evidence that organizations are "shaking it up a little."

On Organizational Impact

Lessons from Hewlett-Packard and Microsoft

HP's Clarke sees "increased management attention at all levels in dealing with 404." Within his own walls, he notes, "we are modifying and substantially increasing the internal controls investment across every function." This includes the very top of the organization, where, Clarke points out: "We are testing this at the board level with more rigorous and, frankly, longer audit committee meetings, as well as doing it at every subfunction in the company."

In terms of the post Sarbanes-Oxley evolution in his own organization, Clarke underscores "increased attention, increased training, and increased formalization of control processes." Like Microsoft, HP makes policy manuals available on its website with required reading and follow-up surveys to ensure compliance. In addition, Clarke stresses, "we're seeing more proactive and reactive testing of audit and control processes." Topping the list, however, says Clarke, is increased engagement. There's no question, he notes, "that we see it higher on the priority list of the day-to-day manager, the day-to-day executive."

It appears that the finance functions of many organizations are themselves leading the charge to promote greater visibility of the extended control function at the executive level. Clarke expounds: "This helps to make it a priority for others deeper in the organization."

Microsoft's Di Valerio would agree: "The business groups at Microsoft really know the Microsoft policies and how revenue and costs flow through our financial statements. But prior to Sarbanes, most had very little interest or interaction with U.S. GAAP or external reporting." That's changing, he says. "Today, they have to have a good sense for both. The leaders of each of the business units are now reading, evaluating, and helping write the MD&A. The business unit CFOs and controllers are now saying, 'What are my internal management reporting statements? What adjustments are being made to convert them into U.S. GAAP? And how do I make sure I understand those changes in order to evaluate and analyze our externally reported results?'"

"On a personal level," HP's Clarke adds, "I spend at least a couple of days a month, a couple of meetings a month, with my head of internal audit. That is probably double what I would have done prior to this increased attention on controls. There is much more dialogue at every business review within HP."

At his Redmond, Washington, office, Di Valerio points to the disclosure committee Microsoft formed in light of Sarbanes-Oxley as a good example of how to take a requirement and turn it into a value-added initiative. "The key," he says, "is really managing the process to get the most out of that committee, and not make it a bureaucracy." Microsoft's group, comprised of individuals from legal, tax, treasury, the controllership, investor relations, marketing, and its seven business unit CFOs, "meets on a quarterly basis to go through the disclosures in our Form 10-Ks and 10-Qs. "The process allows us to discuss comments across the organization and to flag and resolve issues," he says, and adds that members use the group as an active session to update each other on their respective control systems and processes. "They bring up the issues that are paramount to them and their businesses," he says, "to make sure we have a process to address them and accurately characterize them in the documents.

"It's a good meeting," he continues. "We open communication across the business lines and educate the senior business unit executives, the CFOs, and controllers on the overall control structure and the kinds of things they ought to be questioning. And we do so in a manner that allows key concerns and comments to be addressed early on."

Business Risk Controls
Lessons from Omnicom Group
The previous lessons examined internal controls in a financial reporting context. In this example we look at how a

company uses its structure and controls in a broader business-risk context.

Omnicom Group is different than the other companies we've discussed. CEO John Wren has put together an interesting ensemble. Though Omnicom is made up of essentially many self-contained entities, it is clearly not a conglomerate—the different operating units, while largely self-contained, form a single business enterprise—and is much more stable and powerful than merely the sum of the parts. Omnicom companies operate in the disciplines of advertising, marketing services, specialty communications, interactive/digital media, and media buying services. Its clients are located in all key international cities.

Through purposeful development and acquisitions, the company has a built a carefully balanced, distributed-risk environment. First, imagine Omnicom Group's corporate entity as a core object in the center of a circle. Each of its units and clients is distributed around the circle's circumference. And each is connected to the core by a wire. The core's position in the center depends on the net effects of tension, force, and direction. No single wire can be allowed to apply a disproportionate tension, or it pulls the core toward it. The positions on the circumference of units and clients cannot shift disproportionately either, or that too may pull the core away from its center. As a result, if one wire snaps, the core may shift a little, but the other wires keep it from shifting too much. It is like a physical manifestation of portfolio theory, where the tensions and directions have the counterbalancing influence of matched risk correlations.

There is virtually nothing random about Omnicom's universe. To grow, Omnicom adds more clients to the circle and maintains a healthy client/service ratio. To optimize its overall risks, Omnicom intuitively balances client types, locations, and local and global economics. Says Wren: "The nature of our business is largely distributed. We have a large number of relatively small companies and units, so, [with proper balance], when you break those risks down in every one of the units, the real impact to us [corporate] is pretty minimal."

The portfolio of clients is such that none pose a disproportionate business risk, and the Omnicom firms are located in the same cities around the world, thus providing Wren and corporate managers with both a localized and global view of the various disciplines. As a result, says Wren, "while each of our clients and agencies is critically important to us, there's no one place, no one client, that is significant enough to Omnicom that if there were a breakdown it would put the company, or the things we worry about, in serious jeopardy."

The balanced "tension" is Omnicom's way of trying to stay ahead of the risk curve. Wren explains: "First, you have the balance of our services." No single discipline is large enough to dominate how resources are allocated. "The second most important thing is the geographic profile of our portfolio." Here, again, Omnicom strives to ensure that no single client poses a disproportionate business risk in any of its geographies, and that no geography is overexposed by a preponderance of clients. "And third is the competitive nature of our businesses among themselves. We have multiple subsidiaries servicing the same client, but not under the same central leadership." The latter point is interesting, and perhaps unique to a company like Omnicom.

"It's part of the way the company was built," Wren explains. "For example, we have approximately 30 subsidiaries servicing Pfizer. So, we get an awful lot of information about the relationship from multiple independent sources. We know how clients are working with their marketing suppliers and vendors. We know what's going right and what's going wrong in each one of those cases. If an agency who should be bringing information to us isn't forthcoming, there are many siblings who are willing to give us that information."

If it sounds a bit Orwellian, Wren assures us it's not: "It's not done like the secret police. This is all done openly by these companies who are looking out for their own self-interest; and they happen to define their self-interest consistent with Omnicom's self-interest."

Self-interest and culture at Omnicom are inextricably linked and reflected in the balance of autonomy and authority. "Culture is really the root of what distinguishes us from our competitors," says Wren. "Culturally, we're focused, and always have been, on creativity, the integrity of our agencies, and our people. Our decentralized structure combined with a focus on clients has allowed our business to evolve and stay ahead of the competition."

The foci that Wren describes manifest themselves in very different ways among the different entities: "There are strong cultural differences in the way they approach the business, from one operating unit within Omnicom to another, and how they approach a client. That said, though, the basic business fundamentals—the need to protect the creative product and the need to operate with a great deal of integrity—are at the core of every one of those units. And we've seen that consistently played out throughout the entire company. Most of the players that are here have been hand-selected to be here. As we've brought them on board, or acquired them, they've cleared not only the quantitative hurdles, but many qualitative evaluations as well. As I said, this culture is something that was at our core when we were a much smaller company. And we've guarded it very, very closely as we've gotten larger over the years."

Omnicom's financial controls are designed to reduce financial risk while minimally impeding any unit's flexibility. In many ways, the entities have a lot of freedom, even over financial decisions. But there are some qualifications. Wren explains: "We have, for instance, very tight controls globally over our cash management system. We can see on a daily basis whether companies are generating in cash what we're reporting as income. If there's a disparity between income and cash, it's a very early warning signal that there's something that we need to look into."

Income versus cash is just one area of scrutiny: "We also have very tight financial controls on any capital expenditure, or any expenditure, which involves a commitment of more than 12 months. There's a great deal of autonomy within our operating budget, but if there's an expense or an item that's going to be multiyear, that unit has to come to a central source to get that approved." As a result, claims Wren, "there's very little flexibility to mask problems. We can see what's going on pretty clearly from a review of those factors. It points us to things that we should investigate a little further."

With regard to controls over client choice, Wren is again careful to rein in risk without ruling out exceptions. Here again, though, there are qualifications aimed at limiting risks when decisions outside the norm are made. "We're pretty picky about client selection, and we've always been," he states. "We have approximately 5000 clients around the world, and if they're not all global leaders, they're considered blue-chip companies within their countries."

Nevertheless, Wren acknowledges that Omnicom has occasionally allowed for differences. "We let a few exceptions creep in during the dot-com days," he says. But Wren stacked the deck in Omnicom's favor: "We have strict financial controls over who can make financial commitments. So, we were able to say, 'Okay, we don't think you should take this client, but if they're willing to prepay you, and we are not asked to buy another desk, or rent another square foot of space, or hire extra staff, then go ahead and have a ball.'"

Finally, a key success factor in Omnicom's business-risk control environment is the equality it affords to both its operations and financial managers. As Wren puts it: "If you're the CEO or head of a unit, your independence runs to building your client's brand, developing your people, and growing the market share of your agency." He continues: "Our financial folks know that they have a separate responsibility to the corporation to make sure that they're protecting the company's tangible and intangible assets." And he adds: "The financial people in this organization are really treated as equals, not servants of the people running the agencies."

As a result, Wren claims, "because of the separation of duties, a great creative person or a great account person has all the authority in the world to do the best thing for the client or for the office, respectively. But neither person has absolute authority. There is tension that gets created by this separation and equality, and we found it to be pretty healthy."

CONCLUSION

Art Linkletter once remarked: "Things turn out best for the people who make the best out of the way things turn out." Although the press has spread phrases such as "heightened scrutiny," "lapse controls," and "poor accountability" like butter liberally and regularly across many of its internal or business control stories, the executives we spoke with demonstrate that the renewed focus on controls is yielding valuable insights and practices.

CHAPTER 11

Holistic, Integrated Approaches to Risk Management

"It is not necessary to change. Survival is not mandatory."

—W. Edwards Deming

Risk management, traditionally, has segregated and encapsulated specific risks, often applying different approaches and philosophies to each. It has been a static approach, based on a periodic snapshot of risk, leaving everyone guessing in between. The feeling among those we interviewed is that this leads to seeing the trees but missing the forests. The consensus is one that opts for seeing both. As a result, the terms "holistic" and "integrated" frequently punctuated our discussions.

Enterprise risk management (ERM) is a response to the sense of inadequacy in using a silo-based approach to manage increasingly interdependent risks. It's a response to the reputation and market risks—not to mention personal liability risks—associated with managements and boards receiving and then relaying information that is not reasonably accurate. It's a response to the need by all organizations to improve their abilities to increase shareholder and/or stakeholder value.

There is no widely accepted ERM handbook, no shrink-wrapped software solution. ERM lends itself to customized approaches that span from the informal to the very formal, from the centralized to the decentralized.

Richard Bressler notes that formalized risk management practices are much tougher to implement when your business is highly diversified. In a more homogenized environment, he observes, "you can have one set of risk policies or risk management procedures." But, he states, "how do you even start doing that when you have a studio business, a television production business, a radio business, and an outdoor business . . . ?"

Yet, for all that, Viacom has a very strong risk culture. Bressler and fellow management stress setting the right tone at the top and tight internal discipline. "I've actually become a bigger believer," he says, "that one or two people at the top in leadership who conduct themselves in the right way, can affect 100,000 people or can affect the environment that 100,000 people work in." That's why, he concludes, "the easy question is asking what risk is, especially if you look at it holistically like we do. I think the real hard question is how you manage it."

There is tremendous diversity in risk profiles, organizational structures, and cultures, all of which are shaping factors in any ERM implementation decision. But amidst the diversity are discernible common features, many of which we've already examined in other contexts. We will look at a variety of ERM approaches, identifying some common-denominator features. We will also examine more closely risk correlation and risk optimization, which are both important aspects of any ERM approach. Finally, we will look at the individual roles people will be expected to play in any company's ERM scheme.

DOING ERM

Evidence, even if not empirical at this stage in its evolution, suggests that ERM benefits may be significant. For one thing, when volatility is managed, as ERM clearly strives to do, a company's cost of capital is logically improved. Costs are also reduced by directing management's attention and invest-ment to the risks that matter—recognizing that not all do to the same degree—and loosening risk mitigation strategies on those that matter less. Likewise, the joint output of sharper focus and clearer risk correlations can help a company exploit opportunities, even if that opportunity is as elemental as simply outpacing a competitor at the risk management process.

Samsung

Doh Seok Choi, CFO of Korean electronics giant Samsung, says: "Looking back, during my term as CFO, my biggest regret was our failure to control the risks that had resulted from the absence of a reliable risk management system. What we had could not keep up with the rapidly growing company."

He continues: "In the past, risk management primarily depended on the capabilities of each employee in detecting and dealing with potential risks, as we did not have companywide risk management systems and rules in place. But this approach was not up to detecting and preventing these risks as the company began growing at rapid pace."

To remedy the situation, Samsung's CFO "enacted and implemented a policy that created a set of rules to deal with each risk process, and which was managed through a system—an ERM system.

This system lets Samsung define the company's four primary risk categories and establish a system to monitor and evaluate each of their impacts on profitability and other measures. The four risk factors are *strategic, operational, financial,* and *other.* All risk-related information is updated on a regular basis and reported to the rest of the company.

Under strategic risks, Samsung focuses on its investment strategy. Its place in a very cyclical industry, coupled with the need for large capital equipment investments to remain competitive, creates huge risks. "One wrong decision can have disastrous results for the company," states Choi. To manage that risk, the ERM system helps Samsung confine investments to those that can be done with internally generated cash, minimum payback periods, and quarterly reviews.

Financial risks are primarily foreign exchange rate fluctuations and credit risk from overseas accounts. Choi explains: "As a global company, foreign currency denominated transactions make up about 70 percent of total sales, and we have over 70 subsidiaries abroad. Clearly, fluctuations in foreign exchange rates can seriously impact our financial performance." Samsung's ERM enables it to monitor and manage financial risks in real time.

Choi recognizes the risk interrelationships at Samsung: "The company's core R&D, procurement, production, logistics, and operations each have their own processes and risks which are interrelated. One risk can set off another, creating a potential chain reaction of new risks."

Thus, he sees the advantages in treating them as a set rather than individually. "To effectively manage these risks," says Choi, "they must be administered together as one unit [e.g., portfolio management] so that the risks can be minimized in a whole process, and the company's efficiency can be optimized."

The effect, Choi says, "is analogous to an orchestra, which can only present a superior performance if the several different sections perform well as a unit, and together as an orchestra."

Peabody Energy[1]

Peabody Energy is a $2.8 billion St. Louis-based producer and distributor of coal. Usually when we think of energy, we think in terms of electricity producing and distributing companies, or petroleum companies, but there is still a significant amount of coal being mined, refined, and shipped. In fact, the United States is the second largest coal producing nation (China is number one), having delivered one billion tons in 2001 alone.

According to an article on Peabody Energy for *CFO Magazine*, even before Sarbanes-Oxley, Rick Navarre, Peabody's CFO, had developed a sophisticated, comprehensive methodology for analyzing and quantifying risk.[2] He wanted Peabody's audit committee to understand the risks—especially the major ones—confronting the company. On the heels of that effort, Navarre went on to establish a worthy example of ERM.

From the outset, Navarre was inclusive. He queried a dozen Peabody people whose job responsibilities spanned from executive to department manager. He was gathering a bottoms-up view of the risks these people believed were challenging their oversight areas.

The risks described fell naturally into four categories: financial, information technology, operational, and strategic. These were charted using the familiar assessment "likelihood and impact" graph, and the quantification relied on a mix of intuition, experience, and research. For example, says Navarre, "the likelihood of a business interruption is low, but the severity of that event, in terms of monetary risk, would be off the charts."

Peabody's process is completely dynamic. A cross-functional risk management committee has monthly meetings, with Navarre as chairman, to update its risk view. He explains: "If a new risk emerges—say we enter into a joint venture or acquisition—we meet to assess the inherent risks and feed them into the ERM process."

How has ERM helped Peabody? "Instead of looking at individual risks, ERM gives us the ability to assess all the risks of the company and understand them, separately and in relation to each other, potentially identifying risks we may not otherwise have identified, and then making a determination to either mitigate that risk or choose to accept it."

Peabody's audit committee sees great value in the effort. William Rusnack, committee chairman, praises it: "We've learned through this process not only the scope and breadth of risks inherent in the business, but also the various methods that management is using to effectively manage and balance those risks."

Seminole Electric Cooperative[3]

Would ERM serve the needs of a not-for-profit, electrical generation and distribution cooperative? John Geeraerts, financial services vice-president at Tampa-based Seminole Electric Cooperative, thought so, according to the same article in *CFO Magazine*. "We needed to create a broad list of risks facing the company, not just the risks that executive staff had cited, but risks perceived by executives across all corporate lines," Geeraerts explains.[4]

Just as Peabody did, Seminole began by putting together an eight-person, cross-functional committee representing power plant operations, internal audit, tax, and finance. The committee's job was to devise an appropriate questionnaire and distribute it to over 100 other Seminole managers at all levels. Timothy Rogers, Seminole's manager of tax risk and property accounting, calls it "brainstorming across all corporate lines."

Again, the purpose was to gather the bottoms-up risk view. What started as a list of 60 was pared down to a list of 25. Then executive workshops were held to find out what responses, if any, were being taken to mitigate them, and who was accountable for ensuring and monitoring these actions.

The remaining 25 risks were further distilled to produce a top five ranking:

1. Loss of generating capacity

2. Loss of market

3. Optimum mix of power resources

4. Fuel price volatility

5. Regulatory risks

From here the process moved on to assessing, charting, and assembling the risks into a matrix. Though still a work in progress, Seminole's ERM effort has already provided some insights. Geeraerts explains: "For fuel price volatility, the option is a fuel hedging program; for the loss of power lines, the option is insurance; for the risk of terrorism, the option is elevating our security officer to senior staff level."

ERM COMMON DENOMINATORS

At its core, ERM is about helping companies achieve protection from risk and optimizing opportunities. Chiefly, this is exercised by eliminating existing functional, divisional, departmental, and cultural barriers and by aligning strategy, processes, people, and knowledge in their stead. The intent is to shake loose the collective uncertainties the enterprise faces and to shape and mold these to best advantage. In some respects the trend toward ERM represents a philosophical shift. It is the recognition that risk is part of the fabric of value creation. Where traditional risk management has tended to remain codified as protection against financial or physical asset hazards, current thinking recognizes the interrelationship between all main organizational functions and risks.

We could examine many more ERM case histories and find that those efforts that bore fruit had certain common denominators. In the Peabody and Seminole cases, the efforts began with a gathering of bottoms-up risks, that is, the risks that departmental managers identified as those that kept them awake at night.

Although Peabody did the risk gathering, categorizing, and paring in one step, and Seminole did it in two, each established an initial priority ranking. Regardless of whether risk management resources are limited or abundant, apply them to the risks that matter most.

Any ERM, or for that matter, any risk management system, will involve a risk-assessment and risk-response component. This is the place, in the scheme of things, where you assess the risk in likelihood and impact terms, and make an informed risk-response decision. What really separates a good ERM approach from departmental risk management is the ability to allow those bottoms-up risks to bubble to the top and become part of an enterprise portfolio of risks. Here, they can be seen not only in the context of the department or business unit that identified them, but also in the context of all the other risks and the company's business strategy. From that perspective, it is easier to evaluate correlations and total impact and make changes to optimize the risk portfolio. It is also possible to see how the risks, in aggregate, align with the corporation's risk appetite and business strategy.

Implicit in any effective ERM approach is the information technology component. Historical data and current operations data must be accessed, processed, formatted, and distributed. The underlying goal is to make sure the right information goes to the right people at the right time. Doing so is a huge challenge. There are legacy system compatibility and data processing, networking, and security issues. For companies that have made significant digital transformations, these issues may be compounded. On the other hand, there are a handful of companies that offer so-called "business intelligence" or "business performance" systems designed to support nearly all of these underlying functions, such as broad data access, data transformation tools, data display and formatting, network access to the tools, and so on.

One important benefit of ERM is its dynamic, adaptive structure. Effective, comprehensive monitoring and reporting provides the feedback loop necessary to achieve that adaptive quality.

AN ERM FRAMEWORK

As depicted in the chart below, there are four components to the ERM process, each of which is iterative and ongoing.

The process is often analogized to portfolio management. In this way, you might imagine each defined asset exposure as, say, a share in a company. The costs, growth, degree of promise, and likelihood of success all differ widely. As you

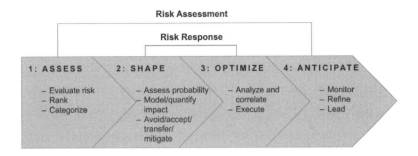

Source: KPMG LLP, 2003.

look at the assemblage of "shares" gathered in your portfolio, you will quickly see that you care about some far more than others. You'll also see that you're invested in some far more than others—in certain cases more than you should be and in other cases less. You'll know this because you will evaluate them using the lens most relevant to your business. You will compare them against whatever metrics are important to your company. You will assess them against the relative maturity of your business. You will peer at them through your company's own culture of risk taking. And you will evaluate them against your standing, both competitive and financial.

RISK CORRELATIONS AND OPTIMIZATIONS

In the early 1950s, economist Harry P. Markowitz introduced portfolio theory, a way of looking at investments as part of a set rather than individually. His premise was that certain stocks tended to move in some degree of lockstep while others tended to move in opposite directions. Correlation, which is by definition comparative, describes the behavior of two stocks relative to one another. A portfolio of stocks that move largely in lockstep—that are positively correlated, for example—will have a much larger volatility than one in which the stocks are either uncorrelated, or negatively correlated (e.g., move in opposite directions). One can therefore adjust the portfolio's volatility by rearranging the amount and types of shares to change the correlations.

Portfolio theory can also be applied to risk portfolios. Similar correlations exist for risks as for securities. For example, a personal computer company has a risk of integrated-circuit shortages, and a risk of competitive oversupply and price degradation. These two risks would be negatively correlated, since if one occurred, the other is much less likely to occur. Using portfolio management concepts, a company's risks can be optimized. Analysis may reveal that one risk can be increased because of the negative correlation with another. Or, in another case, a company that is prepared to avoid a risk may find it complements one that already is accepted or partially shared. Too much focus on risk mitigation rather than risk optimization can result in a company paying more and getting less.

Armed with this information, you may make adjustments to your portfolio. You'll think about things like weight and balance. Are you too heavily concentrated in certain areas of your business? Are investments in high growth/high risk areas counterbalanced with other, more stable avenues? You'll then look to guard certain key assets and related exposures that need protecting, using modeling tools, financing tactics, insurance, and other mitigation techniques.

You'll also identify certain key assets and their related exposure as opportunities that can be exploited, and you will design plans to execute around that—whether it's leveraging some of the same product or geographic concentrations identified earlier to cement a competitive lock hold, or extending hard-won FX expertise in one business unit across other areas of the enterprise.

In tandem with these actions, a viable ERM initiative will encompass the ability to stay alert to change and anticipate economic, regulatory, operational, and other variables that can alter the health of one's portfolio.

Thus, risk management is moving well beyond the tradition of risk mitigation, that of using controls to limit exposure to problems, and moving toward portfolio optimization instead. In so doing, managements are assessing the company's risk appetite and capacity to absorb negative risk events among a group of risks across the enterprise, seizing opportunities within those limits and capitalizing on the rewards that result.

That is the process. How companies formalize it is an individual matter. Fundamentally, however, says CEO Mark Hurd of NCR, "a business's ability to transform data into meaningful streams of information that can lead to a deeper understanding of the organization and its potential vulnerabilities is absolutely essential to successful risk management." He adds: "It's necessary to have in place an enterprise decision-making environment that provides an integrated view of information across the business."

DIVISION OF RESPONSIBILITIES

Organizational approaches to risk management may be centralized at the corporate level or decentralized among divisions or processes, depending on the nature of the risks in question and the organizational preferences of management.

While there is no right or wrong, the KPMG white paper *Understanding Enterprise Risk Management: An Emerging Model for Building Shareholder Value* observes:

☐ Centralized risk management tends to focus on risks that affect the achievement of key corporate objectives and strategies and significantly affect most if not all functions and processes (e.g., reputation management). These risks may be referred to as enterprisewide (EW) risks. Accountability for EW risks may reside with the CEO and the board of directors (although responsibility for EW risks may be dispersed throughout the organization). Other risks that may be managed centrally include those that require specialized skill sets that cannot be duplicated at the division level or those that require partnering or contracting at the corporate level.

☐ Decentralized risk management pushes the responsibility for risk management to those who live with it day to day. Risks that may be best managed in this way are division or process-level risks, which are those that are significant only within a particular process but nonetheless affect the organization's ability to successfully implement its strategies overall.[5]

The internal environment represents the root or foundation of a company's ERM approach. From the internal environment we derive the ERM discipline and structure. It influences and shapes business strategy and objectives, which in turn influence and shape risk strategies. The internal environment is the source of the risk management philosophy. It establishes the enterprisewide risk tolerance or appetite. The creation of every other ERM component is derived from it and obeys its natural laws.

In practice, the internal environment includes the board of directors, corporate and divisional management, right on down to the individual business unit. Its existence begs integration along with clear communications describing the underlying principles and their overarching effect on decisions and actions.

Board of Directors

NCR roots its board level process around its Audit Committee. Says CEO, Mark Hurd: "At each quarterly meeting, members meet to review new risks, make changes in the severity of existing risks, and to determine those risks no longer applicable." Where appropriate, the committee then elevates the issues to the full board of directors. When asked what risk dimensions boards most overlook, Hurd notes: "Too many companies have failed to grasp the implications and potential severity of long-term operational risks to their business. Hindsight may often be 20-20, but in the realm of risk management, foresight needs to be just as clear."

Scott Di Valerio says this about Microsoft's risk management objectives: "The goal is to minimize risk in the most cost-effective way. This translates into minimizing risk related to damage to property, intellectual property, employee risks, control risks, and the like. Here, we take a look at it in a holistic fashion. Intellectual property is key. Our employee base is key, and the overall financial control and integrity is key. These are the three underpinnings, and we design our control and risk management program around them."

With regard to ERM, the board's job is one of oversight. It has to know what management is doing about risk management and assure itself that those efforts are effective. Since risk appetite plays such an important role in risk response decisions, the board must oversee and concur in the CEO's risk-appetite development decisions. To that end, the board must assure itself that the portfolio view of the company's risks are indeed aligned with risk appetite. The board need not be aware of every risk a company faces, but it must be aware of the major risks and be satisfied that each is being effectively managed.

Chief Executive

The CEO is ultimately responsible for a company's risk management. Although various aspects of that responsibility may be delegated, the CEO owns the successes and failures. As the one who "sets the tone at the top," the CEO's ERM responsibilities begin with establishing a positive internal environment, then seeing that all the other components of ERM are put in place.

The CEO must lead and direct senior managers in the shaping of values, principles, and key policies that will underpin the ERM capability. Together, they must also set strategies and objectives, establish broad-based policies, and determine the company's risk appetite and culture.

General McCaffrey comments: "As you put together a plan, you better listen to the dialogue from your most trusted advisers. You must have integrity in the process. If people come in and tell you things you don't want to hear, and the messenger gets shot, the CEO ends up not hearing the full set of risks. You end up perverting the integrity of your information gathering system. People will say, 'Well he's already decided what we're going to do.' So, someone else thinks, 'Any message that causes him discomfort will only lead to my getting fired, or will harm my career prospects.' Clearly, companies and the armed forces don't want that to be the outcome. You have to produce a climate where people think their best judgments will be listened to, if not acted upon."

Senior Managers

There's a cascading downward of authority and accountability from CEO to senior managers, and from senior managers to subordinates. Each senior manager is responsible for risk assessment and risk responses related to his or her business unit's objectives. Subordinates with responsibilities for specific functions or departments will do the same for their spheres of authority. In essence, each manager is accountable to the next level up for his or her piece of the ERM whole, with the buck ultimately stopping at the CEO's desk.

Risk Officers

As we discussed in Chapter 3, *Risk in a Modern Global Business Context,* several corporations have created the role of Chief Risk Officer. Others have assigned similar responsibilities to an existing corporate officer, often the CFO. Regardless, the responsibilities typically include:

☐ Establishing ERM policies, defining roles and responsibilities, and setting implementation goals

☐ Assigning accountability and authority for ERM in the business units

☐ Improving ERM competence and helping managers align risk responses with risk tolerances

☐ Overseeing integration of ERM with other business planning and management activities

☐ Overseeing development of enterprise and business-unit-specific risk tolerances

☐ Helping managers establish control activities

☐ Helping managers develop reporting protocols and monitoring the reporting process

☐ Reporting to the CEO on progress and problems, and recommending needed remedies

Financial Officers

Where a risk officer is in place, with the responsibilities noted in the previous subsection, the financial officers—CFO, Controller, CAO—help in developing the company's plans and budgets, and in tracking and analyzing performance in the context of operations, compliance, and reporting.

Because of their positions in the organization, and the data they "own," they are naturally positioned to conduct monitoring and follow up on actions and decisions.

Internal Auditors

According to the Institute of Internal Auditors (IIA), the scope of internal auditor responsibilities includes risk management and control systems. However, the IIA indicates they should not be primarily responsible for setting up or maintaining the ERM capability.

Internal auditors should be expected to aid both management and an audit committee by monitoring, examining, evaluating, reporting on, and recommending improvements to ERM processes.

THE BENEFIT OF ERM

An ERM initiative is not foolproof. It is a far more customized effort than, say, enterprise resource planning (ERP), and depends far more on the people part of the technology-people-policies equation than more mature business systems.

But in our effort, in an uncertain world, to minimize the surprise and damage done by risks of the negative persuasion, and to maximize the gains due to risks of the positive persuasion, a reliable crystal ball appears to be the only tangible alternative to ERM.

Prior to Sarbanes-Oxley, no groundswell of companies had been adapting ERM. Without the pressures of the new legislation, the cost-benefit analysis was apparently not compelling enough. Ironically, companies are now more predisposed to ERM in large part because of the data gathering and compliance disciplines imposed by it. But we believe ERM merits another cost-benefit evaluation, and among the benefits evaluators should include are:

☐ Aligning business strategy with risk appetite

☐ Relating growth with risk and return

☐ Improving risk-response decisions

☐ Reducing operational risk surprise and loss

☐ Identifying and managing risks that go cross-enterprise

☐ Integrating responses to multiple risks

☐ Identifying and responding to positive risk opportunities

☐ Improving capital rationalization

CHAPTER 12

The End
of the Beginning

"This is not the end. It is not even the beginning of the end. But, it is, perhaps, the end of the beginning."

—Sir Winston Churchill

You have made it this far, and you're primed to bring an educated risk sensitivity into your organization. Except now you must actually apply it, or at least so we hope. Except also that an unmanaged risk has just reached your desk, your voice mail is full, important reports await your attention, and your assistant has just filled your last open slot this month.

Our days are full of urgent things. That's the job. There's not a thing you touch that doesn't involve strategic gambles, bets chosen, trade-offs made. Therein lies the risk. It's what you're left with after sifting through the stuff of everyday life, the life of a business manager, and seeing what pattern the grains formed and how the gambles worked out, and figuring out whether you were surprised and what you would do differently. How do you encapsulate something so ubiquitous? In some respects, you could say it's like teaching someone how to manage.

The reasoning used to be that you couldn't, that the only way to learn how to manage was to manage. Yet, Harvard, Stanford, Wharton, Duke, and their brethren counter otherwise. They take that seemingly ubiquitous subject and raise awareness of the major issues, requirements, and sources of trouble for their students. They teach those who come to them what to look out for and how to deal with it.

That is also our goal. Consider this summary the open-book final, with no grade, just the opportunity to learn and to improve.

Rod Eddington, CEO of British Airways, puts it well when he says: "I think shareholders will not invest in companies that they think don't take risk management seriously. I call it the health and hygiene factor. Organizations which don't think through these issues and have sensible risk mitigation plans in place will be companies that shareholders naturally shy away from. So, it's not as if they mark you up, necessarily, they just might not include you in the game."

BOARD ACTIVITIES

Good governance implies good risk oversight. Map your key risks. Compare these against management's own presentation. Talk about risk treatments—which to avoid, accept, transfer, or mitigate. When and how should important risks be addressed? For example, do you have undue geographical concentration? What measures should you use to find out?

How do you respond if you do? Do you hedge some of the exposure? There may be no answer, but the questions have to be raised and key risks given serious thought.

Each year, schedule at least one full board meeting, or better yet, an off-site, to serve as a strategic risk summit. Talk about the "big" risks. Think about the near-term risks and the long-term risks. If the issues are not complex, you're not getting to their heart. This should feel like hard work. Note the facts and get somebody to work out the business case.

Understand how much strategic, financial, and operational risk your organization is taking. Determine whether it is satisfactorily positioned to take that level. Consider also if it is overly risk averse. Are opportunities being missed? Be honest about what you know and what you need help in learning. For example, does the board understand the nature and type of financial instruments being used? If not, get educated.

Figure out who owns what risk classes. Who is ultimately responsible for financial risk in your organization? What linkage is there between that person and your head of operations, your CIO, your VP of public affairs? For some organizations, the best response will be a formalized process, for others, something more informal. Still, the board needs to know whom to call and where to get a second opinion.

To consider:

☐ Provide risk education at the board level.

☐ Establish buy-in at the board level for risk appetite and risk strategy.

☐ Review your governance structure.

☐ Develop ownership of risk management oversight by the board.

☐ Review a risk report of the enterprise.

MANAGEMENT ACTIVITIES

What were last year's biggest hurdles and how did they work out? Think about a postmortem. For example, did the systems implementation save you the promised 5 percent, or did the rollout unveil other issues that changed the scope and cost? What did you learn?

Examine your enterprise risk management effort. Do you feel comfortable with its findings? Are there correlations between any weaknesses found and other soft spots in the organization? Is there an opportunity for some classes of risk to be treated once systemically, such as through the use of enhanced policy procedures or documentation requirements?

Sit down with your CFO. See if what you think of as risk matches what he or she thinks of as risk. Be disciplined. We are most of all optimistic. A new idea or promising innovation is exciting. We nearly will it into being. Make sure someone is thinking about the downside. For every large change, make sure someone has come up with a good exit plan. Recognize that the law of averages means that you will need that exit plan on more than one occasion. Make sure it works.

Rely on process and policy to support you in this. As Bob Dellinger of Sprint notes: "Probably the biggest risk that companies face is themselves. Businesses get hooked on certain things. They get hooked on a certain type of technology, or a certain business model, and they miss big, fundamental changes in their industry. They get overly confident about the way they do things." You need to look ahead, and be prepared for and predict change. Agility and speed do matter. Stay flexible and alert and you should be able to manage most risk and most industry changes.

Share meaningful information, internally and with your shareholders. Look at your disclosure process. Are the risks disclosed the same as those that keep you awake? Your investors are interested in you because of your proven ability to execute. Messaging is important. It's not just "full disclosure," as the much-bandied phrase suggests. It's giving, as Robert Woods of P&O puts it, "plenty of good steers." Mainly, it's about anticipating, responding, and holding yourself responsible.

To consider:

☐ Assess your company's risk tolerance.

☐ Create a high-level risk policy aligned with strategic business objectives.

☐ Create a risk management organizational structure and ensure clear reporting lines.

☐ Develop and assign responsibilities for risk management.

☐ Communicate board vision, strategy, policy, responsibilities, and reporting lines to all employees across the organization.

☐ Involve stakeholders and the investment community.

ESTABLISH A COMMON RISK CULTURE

Risk nomenclature varies widely. If you're talking "strategic risk" and somebody else is hearing "process risk," will you have a problem? We interviewed a number of executives for this book, and each of them had a different definition of risk, each one thoughtful, each one correct, but each one certainly representing a different perspective. As dull as it may conceivably seem, write it down. Break out the important categories affecting your organization and let people know how you think about them.

Risk is everyone's responsibility. Sarbanes-Oxley, Enron, and related events have certainly made most employees far more attuned to the subject than probably ever before. Let everyone know that they own their part of the risk of doing business. For some organizations, it may make sense for nonofficers to "sign off" on their reports up through the chain of command. For other organizations, a different procedure may work better. Some companies are even moving to place risk management activities directly within an employee or manager's performance requirement and incorporating risk concepts into personal goals.

Contemporary management tells us that organizations run more effectively with an empowered employee base. This means ownership for taking the educated gambles, and ownership for seeing the process through, whatever the outcome. Failure happens, but credibility prevails when you have a process supporting your attempts to do the right thing.

Failure happens less frequently when the right mix of resources is brought to the task. Think about whether and how your company's risk culture inclines employees to act. Is there balance? In the risk-reward equation, does your culture stress a manager's risk responsibilities with the same determination as it does the manager's reward or earnings generation responsibilities? Do departments like Internal Audit feature subject matter experts in the right fields? Is further training needed? Consistency across the global enterprise is important in leveraging knowledge and in aligning approaches.

To consider:

☐ Use common risk language and concepts.

☐ Communicate about risk using appropriate channels and technology.

☐ Develop training programs for risk management.

☐ Empower managers with defined risk boundaries.

☐ Identify and train risk experts.

☐ Align risk management techniques with company culture.

☐ Develop a knowledge sharing system.

☐ Include risk management activities in job descriptions.

EMBED, MEASURE, AND MONITOR

There is no beginning and no end. Risk management is necessarily dynamic and evolutionary, or at least it should be. For this to be the case, people need to know about it. Align and integrate risk management activities within business processes. Embed real-time controls related to risk in your automated systems. Establish a good feedback loop.

Think about it. What happens when a key process goes down? Some contingency is probably in place. Somebody is probably alerted. But who else hears about it? Who should hear about it? Does the process get refined as a consequence? How would you know? For critical processes, be they strategic, financial, or operational, chart the major metrics and highlight possible trouble spots. Make sure important infrastructure is up-to-date. Then provide a regular reporting mechanism to measure performance relative to these metrics.

Benchmark against other companies in your class. Benchmark potential incidents against companies that have weathered the same things. When Microsoft was studying the possible impact of an earthquake on their business, they looked at the most recent catastrophic example that they could find—Kobe Steel. Then they went out to Kobe and talked to people at that company to find out what they had learned from the experience. They asked them what they did differently as a result to help their business recover strategically. Brent Callinicos, Microsoft's treasurer, states: "We learned a lot as a result of digging into that and it changed the way we bought insurance." This is a perfect example of risk optimization.

Unlike the classroom, you can and should peer over your shoulder at the competitor working next to you. The old maxim, "If it ain't broke, don't fix it," doesn't apply. Some companies "break" their system deliberately. By testing, studying, and refining, they hope to catch any serious weaknesses before somebody else beats them to it.

To consider:

☐ Identify key performance indicators and critical success factors related to risk.

☐ Establish success measures for risk strategy and activities.

☐ Provide a periodic process for measuring risk and return.

☐ Identify and implement monitoring processes and methods of feedback.

☐ Establish a feedback loop and replace outmoded systems as needed.

CONCLUSION

All organizational change starts at the top. For it to happen, the CEO and the board must be committed to it. Fundamentally, they must believe that the change leads to value. Does risk management equate? Unquestionably it does. The practice of risk management has emerged as critical to value creation. It offers shareholders better stability, better predictability, and better scrutability. For a company wishing to operate at the top of its class, it stands to reason that as all business involves risk, the management of risk should involve every aspect of the business itself.

Recognition

We are extremely grateful to KPMG LLP's Audit and Risk Advisory Services for sharing with us their excellent papers:

"A New Focus on Governance: Managing Stakeholder Expectations to Sustain Business Value"

"Beyond Numbers: How Leading Organizations Link Values with Value to Gain Competitive Advantage"

"New Strategies and Best Practices in Internal Audit: An Emerging Model for Building Organisational Value Focusing on Risk"

"Understanding Enterprise Risk Management: An Emerging Model for Building Shareholder Value"

We are extremely grateful to KPMG LLP's Audit Committee Institute for making available their research, presentations, surveys, and papers, including:

"Reflecting on the Past; Focusing on the Future"

"Building a Framework for Effective Audit Committee Oversight—Fall 2002 and Spring 2003 Roundtable Reports and Panel Notes"

"Audit Committee Basic Principles"

"Audit Committee Updates"

We acknowledge with extreme gratitude KPMG LLP's Department of Professional Practice for their review and support as well as for such superb material as:

"Defining Issues"

"Sarbanes-Oxley: A Closer Look"

"Sarbanes-Oxley Management Section 404: Assessment of Internal Control and the Proposed Auditing Standards"

Thanks finally to KPMG LLP's Internal Audit Services practice for sharing their study, "Internal Audit: Reassessing the Value."

Bibliography

Banham, Russ, "Fear Factor," *CFO Magazine,* June 2003.

Barings Bank, case study, ERisk.com.

Barton, Thomas and William G. Shenkir. *Making Enterprise Risk Management Pay Off.* Financial Times Prentice Hall, 2002.

Bausch and Lomb information, http://www.bausch.com/us/vision/about/story.jsp.

Bell, Timothy. *Auditing Organizations Through A Strategic-Systems Lens.* KPMG Business Measurement Process, 1997.

Bell, Timothy. *Cases in Strategic-Systems Auditing.* KPMG and University of Illinois at Urbana-Champaign, Business Measurement Case Development and Research Program, 2002.

Bernstein, Peter L. *Against the Gods, the Remarkable Story of Risk.* John Wiley & Sons, 1996.

Berube, Gerard, "Uncertain Balance," *CA Magazine,* Canadian Institute of Chartered Accountants, 1997.

Boer, Peter F, "Real Options: The IT Investment Risk-Buster," *Optimize Magazine,* July 2002.

Borge, Dan. *The Book of Risk.* John Wiley & Sons, 2001.

"Budgeting for Risk," ERisk.com, March 2002.

BusinessWeek Online, News Analysis, "Even in Retreat, Jack Welch Leads," September 18, 2002.

Byrne, John, "At Enron, the Environment Was Ripe for Abuse," *BusinessWeek*, February 25, 2002.

Byrne, Rebecca, "What did they know? What did they understand?," The Street.com, July 2, 2003.

Charan, Ram and Jerry Useeum, "Why Companies Fail," *Fortune*, May 15, 2002.

Ciccarelli, Maura C, "Degrees of Preparation," *Risk & Insurance*, March 3, 2003.

Conger, Jay and Edward E Lawler. *Corporate Boards: New Strategies for Adding Value at the Top.* Jossey-Bass, 2001.

"Corporate Governance and Culture," World Economic Forum, January 24, 2003.

"Corporate Governance: The New Strategic Imperative," KPMG LLP, Assurance and Advisory Services, 2002.

Couhy, Michel; Dan Galai; and Robert Mark. *Risk Management.* McGraw-Hill, 2001.

Cunningham, Lawrence A., "Preventive Corporate Lawyering: Averting Accounting Scandals," *Introductory Accounting and Finance for Lawyers,* West Law School, 3rd Edition, May 2002.

Daiwa Bank, case study, ERisk.com.

"Defining Issues, Final Rules on Internal Control Reporting and Officer Certifications," KPMG LLP, Department of Professional Practice, June 2003.

Derivative Primer. Derivatives Study Center, Washington, D.C.

Drake, Lawrence L, "What your CEO wants to know about managing risk," *Financial Executive,* September 19, 1997.

Euromoney Institutional Investor, "Getting to grips with risk in your business," *Corporate Finance*, November, 2002.

Frankel, Marc T., Ph.D., "Strategy, Risk, and the Way Forward," *The CEO Refresher*, 2003.

Frankel, Marc T., "Strategy, Risk, and the Way Forward," *The CEO Refresher*, 2003.

FRBSF Economic Letter, No. 2002-02, January 25, 2002.

Greenspan, Alan, "Remarks by Federal Reserve Board Chairman Alan Greenspan to the Council on Foreign Relations," *Federal News Service*, November 19, 2002.

Guthrie, Vernon H.; David A. Walker; and Bert N. Macesker, "Enterprise Risk Management," 17th International System Safety Conference, 2002.

Hanley, Mike, CFO.com, March 20, 2002.

Harvard Business School, "Tiffany & Co.—1993," case study, June 9, 1995.

Hawkesby, Christian, "A primer on derivatives markets," Reserve Bank of New Zealand, Bulletin vol. 62, no. 2.

Hillson, David, "Know Your Business Risk, " Strategic Risk, www.strategicrisk.co.uk, April 2003.

Industry Week.com, February 1, 1999.

Johnson, Brandt, "Silver Lining to Tech Stock Clouds?" *Treasury & Risk Management*, May/June 2002.

Johnsson, Margaret and Kim Roll-Wallace, "Expected Costs for Implementing Sarbanes-Oxley Section 404," Financial Executives International, October 8, 2003.

J. P. Morgan, "Credit Derivatives: A Primer," February 1998.

Katz, David M., "What's Your Risk Metric?" CFO.com, July 12, 2001.

Kersten, Denise, "CEOs share their secrets to success," *USA Today,* November 14, 2002.

Kloman, H. Felix, "Enterprise Risk Management: Past, Present and Future," *Risk Management Reports*, vol. 30, no. 5, May 2003.

Kloman, H. Felix, "Paralysis of Uncertainty," *Risk Management Reports*, April 2003.

Koller, Glenn. *Risk Assessment and Decision Making in Business and Industry.* CRC Press, 1999

KPMG, Assurance and Advisory Services Center, KPMG LLP, 2002:

"A New Focus on Governance: Managing Stakeholder Expectations to Sustain Business Value"

"Beyond Numbers: How Leading Organizations Link Values with Value to Gain Competitive Advantage"

"Internal Audit: Reassessing the Value"

"Understanding Enterprise Risk Management: An Emerging Model for Building Shareholder Value"

KPMG, Audit Committee Institute:

"Basic Principles," KPMG LLP.

"Building a Framework for Effective Audit Committee Oversight—Fall 2002 and Spring 2003 Roundtable Reports and Panel Notes." KPMG LLP, 2002, 2003.

"Reflecting on the Past; Focusing on the Future," KPMG LLP, 2003.

KPMG, Department of Professional Practice, KPMG LLP, 2003:

"Sarbanes-Oxley: A Closer Look"

"Sarbanes-Oxley Section 404: Management Assessment of Internal Control and the Proposed Auditing Standards"

KPMG, Management Assurance Services, "New Strategies and Best Practices in Internal Audit: An Emerging Model for Building Organizational Value Focusing on Risk," KPMG LLP, 2001.

Lam, James, "Custom-Built for Success," *Enterprise-wide Risk Management Supplement,* November 1997.

Lam, James, "Enterprise-wide Risk Management and the Role of the Chief Risk Officer, " ERisk.com, March 25, 2000.

Leland, Hayne E. and Mark Rubinstein, "The Evolution of Portfolio Insurance," *Dynamic Hedging: A Guide to Portfolio Insurance,* John Wiley & Sons, 1988.

Leone, Marie, "Your Finance Department Is Second-Rate," CFO.com, February 20, 2003.

"Managing Risk," Office of Government Commerce, UK, 2001.

Marshall, Jeffrey and Ellen M. Heffes, "For CFOs, the to-do list lengthens," *Financial Executive,* November 1, 2002.

Mausser, Helmut and Dan Rosen, "Applying Scenario Optimization to Portfolio Credit Risk," *Algo Research Quarterly,* vol. 2, no. 2, June 1999.

McCarthy, Mary Pat and Jeff Stein, with Rob Brownstein. *Agile Business for Fragile Times.* McGraw-Hill, 2002.

McCarthy, Mary Pat and Keyur Patel. *Digital Transformation.* McGraw-Hill, 2000.

McCarthy, Mary Pat and Stuart Campbell, with Rob Brownstein. *Security Transformation.* McGraw-Hill, 2001.

McKinsey & Co., "Global Investor Opinion Survey: Key Findings," July 2002.

McNamee, David, "A New Approach to Business Risk," *Business Control Magazine,* June/July 1994.

Miccolis, Jerry and Samir Shah, "Enterprise Risk Management: An Analytic Approach," Tillinghast—Towers Perrin, January, 2000.

Miller, Charlene, "The Need for Educated Change in the Boardroom," www.larta.org., November 4, 2002.

Moody, Michael J., "Corporate Governance Moves to the Front Burner," *Rough Notes,* October 2002.

Muermann, Alexander and Ulku Oktem. *The Near-Miss Management of Operational Risk.* The Wharton School, University of Pennsylvania, 2002.

Nagel, Karl, "Auditing Standards," PCAOB Online, originally run in *Compliance Week,* April 24, 2003.

Nussbaum, Bruce, "Why the world needs new thinking," *BusinessWeek,* August 26, 2002.

Peters, Edgar E. *Complexity, Risk, and Financial Markets.* John Wiley & Sons, 1999.

Pezier, Jacques, "Operational Risk Management," ISMA Discussion Papers in Finance, 2002-21, September 2002.

Preston, Sharalyn, "Establishing an Integrated Enterprise Risk Management Solution," University of Memphis presentation, September, 2002.

Rezaee, Zabihollah, "The Six-legged Stool; High-Quality Financial Reporting," *Strategic Finance,* Institute of Management Accountants, February 1, 2003.

Rutan, Stephen A., "The Success Zone: Aligning Your Business Model and Risk Profile," Center for Simplified

Strategic Planning, Inc., http://www.strategyletter.com/ CD0702/featured_article.html.

SEC Release No. 33-8238, Management's Report on Internal Control Over Financial Reporting and Certification of Disclosure in Exchange Act Periodic Reports, June 5, 2003.

Sellers, Patricia, "Coke: Who's in charge here?," *Fortune*, December 9, 2001.

Sharpe, William. *Portfolio Theory & Capital Markets.* McGraw-Hill, 1970.

Stokes, Malcolm, "Total Risk Profiling, The Risk Management Dream Becomes a Reality," Zurich Financial Services Group, 2000.

Sooran, Chand, "Derivatives Explained," Victory Risk Management Consulting, Inc.

Sooran, Chand, "Measuring Risk," Victory Risk Management Consulting, Inc.

Sooran, Chand, "What is Hedging? Why Do Companies hedge?" Victory Risk Management Consulting, Inc.

Thornton, Emily, "A yardstick for corporate risk," *Business Week*, August 26, 2002.

Toevs, Alden L, "Negotiating the Risk Mosaic," presentation by the Risk Management Association, Annual Conference on Capital Management, April 9, 2003.

Tversky, Amos and Daniel Kahneman, "Advances in Prospect Theory: Cumulative Representation of Uncertainty," *Journal of Risk and Uncertainty*, vol.5, no. 4.

Quinn, Lawrence R, "Strengthening the role of the audit committee," *Strategic Finance*, December 2002.

Watkins, Thayer, "Corporate Strategies Toward Foreign Currency Transaction Risk," San Jose State University Economics Department, 1997.

Welch, Scott, "Managing Single-Stock Risk: Unlocking Liquidity with High Net Worth Clients," *Journal of Financial Service Professionals*, September 2000.

Wood, Duncan, "From cop to CRO," ERisk.com, March 2002.

Endnotes

Chapter 3

1. Peter L. Bernstein. *Against the Gods, the Remarkable Story of Risk.* John Wiley & Sons, 1996.

2. Industry Week.com, February 1, 1999.

3. Hans Geiger, "Case 1, Barings Bank," Seminar zur Bank-BWL, November 22, 2000.

4. "Business: The Economy, How Leeson Broke the Bank," BBC News, June 22, 1999.

5. "Crunch Time for Barings," BBC News, November 20, 2000, http://news.bbc.co.uk/1/hi/business/1031427.stm

6. *In re Cendant Corporation Securities Litigation,* 139 F. Supp. 2d 585 (D.N.J. 2001); *In re Cendant Corporation Securities Litigation,*109 F. Supp. 2d 235, (D.N.J. 2000). Brian Graney, "Revisiting Cendant," The Motley Fool.com, January 22, 2001; *The CPA Journal,* December 2002, vol. 72, no. 12; John Cassidy, "The World of Business, the Greed Cycle: How the Financial System Encouraged Corporations to Go Crazy," *The New Yorker,* September 23, 2002.

7. *In re Cendant Corporation Securities Litigation,* 139 F. Supp. 2d 585 (D.N.J. 2001); *In re Cendant Corporation Securities Litigation,* 109 F. Supp. 2d 235, (D.N.J. 2000);

James Surowiecki, "The Multi-Million-Dollar Wages of Sin," MSN Moneybox, July 29, 1998.

8. "Cendant Strikes Out Anew," CNN Money, November 20, 1998.

9. SEC Release No. 39329, Accounting and Auditing Enforcement Release No. 987, November 17, 1997 (imposing a cease and desist order against Bausch and Lomb); Bausch & Lomb Case Study, ERisk.com

10. http://www.bausch.com/us/vision/about/story.jsp

11. Ibid, SEC Release No. 39329.

12. Ibid.

13. Dan Borge. *The Book of Risk*. John Wiley & Sons, 2001.

14. Amos Tversky and Daniel Kahneman, "Advances in Prospect Theory, Cumulative Representation of Uncertainty," *Journal of Risk and Uncertainty*, vol. 5, no. 4, 1992.

15. Ibid, Peter Bernstein.

16. Mike Hanley, CFO.com, March 20, 2002.

17. Ibid.

18. Dr David Hillson, "The Way to Survive—Know Your Business Risks," PM Professional Solutions, www.PM Professional.com

19. David McNamee, "A New Approach to Business Risk," *Business Control Magazine*, June/July 1994.

20. Sharalyn Preston, "Establishing an Integrated Enterprise Risk Management Solution," KPMG LLP, April 2002.

21. Anthony Storr, *Feet of Clay*. Free Press, 1997.

Chapter 4

1. Kovatch, Karen. "ServiceWare backs off of IPO plan in the face of Wall Street uncertainties," Pittsburgh Business Times, October 12, 1992. http://www.bizjournals.com/pittsburgh/stories/1998/10/12/story4.html

2. "Starbucks—Should They Rule?" *Supermarket Guru,* April 26, 2003.

3. "M&M Candies," Food Reference Web site, Food History.

4. *Awake!,* Watch Tower Bible and Tract Society of Pennsylvania, February 22, 2001.

5. *Derivative Primer,* Derivatives Study Center, Washington, D.C., 1999.

6. This statement was made in August 2003, and reflects the currency situation at that time.

7. Dan Borge. *The Book of Risk.* John Wiley & Sons, 2001.

Chapter 5

1. A.P. Hill and Steven Crane, "Treasury and Risk Management," CFO.com, December 12, 2001.

2. Ibid.

3. Thayer Watkins, "FMC," case study, San Jose State University, Department of Economics, http://www2.sjsu.edu/faculty/watkins/tran.htm#FMC

4. Abe De Ramos, "The Perfect Treasury" CFO Asia, April 1, 2002.

5. Alan Greenspan, "International Financial Risk Management," remarks before the Council on Foreign Relations, November 19, 2002.

6. Ibid.

Chapter 6

1. FRBSF Economic Letter, no. 2002-02, January 25, 2002.

2. Columbia Accident Investigation Board, Final Report, August 26, 2003.

3. Daiwa Bank, case study, ERisk.com

4. "Japan's $1-Billion Scam," Asia Week.com, Oct. 27, 1995.

5. Mary Jo White, United States Attorney for the Southern District of New York, press release announcing criminal indictment of Daiwa Bank, November, 2, 1995.

6. "Regulators Terminate the U.S. Operations of Daiwa Bank, Ltd., Japan," press release, Federal Deposit Insurance Corporation, November 2, 1995.

7. Jacques Pezier, "Operational Risk Management," ISMA Discussion Papers in Finance 2002-21, September 2002.

8. Alexander Muermann and Ulku Oktem. *The Near-Miss Management of Operational Risk.* The Wharton School, University of Pennsylvania, 2002.

Chapter 7

1. "Global Investor Opinion Survey: Key Findings," McKinsey & Co., July 2002.

2. Excerpted from "A New Focus on Governance: Managing Stakeholder Expectations to Sustain Business Value," KPMG Management Assurance Services and KPMG Assurance and Advisory Services Center, 2002.

3. Gray Cary Website, Corporate Governance, "New Approaches to Compensation Committees and Executive Compensation" http://www.gcwf.com/gcc/GrayCary-C/Practice-A/CorpGov/cgcompco.doc_cvt.htm

4. Investor Relations Financial Reports, 2003 Proxy Statement, Dow Chemical Corporation, http://www.dow.com/financial/2003prox/board/

5. Corporate Board and Governance Practices, Praxair Corporation, http://www.praxair.com/praxair.nsf/0/e2f fd130ca1a2a5e85256ce80069a27a?OpenDocument

6. Investor Relations, Fleet Boston Financial. "FleetBoston Financial Corporate Corporate Governance Principles," http://www.fleetbank.com/about_companyinforma tion_governance.asp.

7. "Global Investor Opinion Survey: Key Findings," McKinsey & Co., July 2002.

Chapter 8

1. "Interview with Raymond S. Troubh," *Directors Monthly*, National Association of Corporate Directors, June 2003.

2. "Board Members Facing Public Scrutiny Should Bone Up on Finance, Accounting," Wharton School of Business, University of Pennsylvania, http://knowledge.wharton. upenn.edu/

3. John Engen, "Tyco Director Says, 'I've Fallen Off the Cliff, '" *Corporate Board Member,* Special Legal Issue, 2003.

4. Paul S. Atkins, "Speech by SEC Commissioner: Remarks at ALI-ABA Course of Study," SEC, January 9, 2003. http://www.sec.gov/news/speech/spch010903psa.htm

Chapter 9

1. The aggregate market value of the voting and nonvoting common equity held by nonaffiliates.

2. Alan L. Beller, "Speech by SEC Staff: Remarks before the American Bar Association's 2003 Conference for Corporate Counsel," U.S. Securities and Exchange Commission.

3. "Sarbanes-Oxley Section 404: Management Assessment of Internal Control and the Proposed Auditing Standards," KPMG LLP, March 2003.

4. Ibid.

5. Margaret Johnsson and Kim Roll-Wallace, "Expected Costs for Implementing Sarbanes-Oxley Section 404."

Chapter 10

1. *Management's Report on Internal Control Over Financial Reporting and Certification of Disclosure in Exchange Act Periodic Reports,* SEC Release No. 33-8238, June 5, 2003, available at http://www.sec.gov/rules/final/33-8238.htm

Chapter 11

1. Russ Banham, " Fear Factor," *CFO Magazine,* June 2003.

2. Ibid.

3. Ibid.

4. Ibid.

5. "Understanding Enterprise Risk Management: An Emerging Model for Building Shareholder Value," KPMG, Assurance and Advisory Services Center, KPMG LLP, 2002.

Index